Success in Finances

TOMMY FRANKS, PH.D.

SUCCESS IN FINANCES

MONEY MATTERS

2008

Success in Finances

CONTENTS

I Dedicate These Writings Success In Finances To All Individuals That Want A Better And More Productive Life In The Area Of Finances. This Book Will Assist You In Making A Difference In Your Money Habits...Wealth Accumulation...Prosperity...And Greater Success In Your Accomplishments. I Believe That You Are On The Cutting Edge Of Something Big.

FORWARD

Success in Finances by Tommy Franks is an essay that many will find helpful in understanding precepts of God's view of blessings as well as skills in handling what God provides. Listen to what God has to say about the proper management of life resources. Dr. Franks' insights will be difficult for some people, but to those faithful to the Bible, it will be refreshing to read his thoughts on what makes the good steward.

In these first years of the 21st century the entire world is trapped in the addiction of excesses. We want more. We extend our credit until we become slaves to those we owe instead of faithful sons and daughters of God. We have very little savings and the principles of the tithe and gifts to God falls on ears that no longer hear. Our motto has become "spend!" It is this addiction that blinds people from the Word of God. This ruins marriages, relationships, and sets people off on courses of destruction. We have lost the ability to be frugal and faithful.

So, if you are looking for answers and you are tired of being a child of debt instead of a child of God, this material will be very helpful to you.

Dr. Franks' inspires us with his witness and his enthusiasm in a subject that he knows all too well and a subject which he has mastered and, unlike much of the world, one which has not mastered him.

Read and learn...!

The Rev. Dr. Al W. Jenkins
Rector of All Saints' Episcopal Church
Lakeland, Florida

INTRODUCTION

You can get out of debt. You can have more than enough. You can be rich. You can have it all. You do not have to be a slave to poverty, overdue bills, or lack of money. What is the secret? Read this book. YOU deserve the very BEST that life has to offer. You can save money. You can have a good retirement. YOU can be happy and healthy. God wants you to have the necessary resources to "put you over in life". Our Father wants you to have plenty…more than enough. YOU are the BEST product that Heaven has ever produced. You are made in God's image.

MONEY…WEALTH…PROSPERITY…SUCCESS…are yours now. Our loving Father wants you to have plenty…more than enough. Money is on your side. Money is for you…not against you. You can have sweet success in finances. You can be a part of something BIG…"God has given you the power to get WEALTH that He may establish His covenant on earth" (Deut.8:18). Our Father owns all the gold and silver there is. He owns ALL the cattle. He owns all the oil and mineral resources. He wants to share this wealth with us. We must begin to think BIG. God is not a small God. He does not think small.

Financial success is for EVERY person who can receive it. We give and it is given unto us. We must also learn how to receive the blessings that are offered to us. This book is not for the individual who wants to continue to be poor or just barely getting by. BUT it is for the person who desires to have abundance…more than enough. Our provisions come to us daily by the God of the universe. I am talking about plenty. I am talking about "more than enough".

The problem with so many of us today is…we think too small. Did you know there is enough wealth right now on this earth for every living human being on the face of this planet to be a millionaire with money to spare? Literally, the wealth of the earth and financial resources have barely been touched. Where is this money? Some of the money is in the hands of the greedy. Some is in the hands of the covetous ones. Others have selfishly horded gobs of money (billions) of dollars upon themselves. The money is still here. The resources are here. So, what is the problem? Well, a lot of it is in the wrong hands. The wrong people have it. However, there is transference of wealth taking place today. That's where you and I come in. Our responsibility is to receive these monies and then rightly disperse them into God's Kingdom, our families, the Church, the needy, poor, and hungry…for the furtherance of the Gospel. God's abundance is laid up for the just ones…His kids.

MONEY is a very dear subject to all of us. It is even more important to God. Now, some of you may say, "Let me pray about this." Some things we do not have to pray about. For example, the Word says for us to pay tithes. We do not have to pray to find out if it is the Will of God for us to pay tithes. Neither do we have to pray to find out if it is God's will for us to be holy. We do not have to pray to find out if it is the Will of God for us to be baptized. Was Jesus baptized? Yes. If the Word says for us to do or be something, then we simply need to do it. Let us not waste God's time by asking Him something that His Word has already commanded us to do. We can and should fulfill God's covenant by being a channel of His wealth and resources on Planet Earth. The Word says, "Though the wicked shall heap up silver as the dust…the innocent shall divide the silver" (Job 27:16-17). We are the innocent ones (God's children).

We need to be involved in finances. The world's system has had it long enough. The world's system is bankrupt. NOW is the time for YOU and me to get smart about finances and wealth. Our loving Father has already given us the POWER to appropriate this wealth; however, He leaves the choice up to us.

As I have said so many times before, "We are the best product that heaven has ever produced. We are the APPLE of God's eye. The abundance of God will come to you as you accept your responsibility in the Kingdom of God. Freedom of lack…Freedom of worry…Freedom to excel has come to you and your family through Jesus Christ. God has anointed you by His Holy Spirit. Man can not stop you. No one can stop you. You are the only person that can stop you from God's best. You are strong and you can live long. YOU are in the hollow of God's hand. The yoke of poverty has been destroyed from your life. FINANCES in abundance belong to YOU NOW.

We are children of the light and not darkness. We need to commit ourselves to receive God's wealth and to assist Him in establishing His covenant (Will) across this land. We must start seeing ourselves as God sees us...whole, wealthy, bold, powerful, and more than a conqueror. This earth belongs to God and HIS children. We are HIS sons and daughters. As His kids, we should have more than enough so that we in turn...can give to our families, local church, share with others, and plant seed into the Kingdom of God.

"The wealth of the sinner is laid up for the JUST" (Pr.13:22). Who are the Just Ones? The Just ones are the righteous ones on Planet Earth. They are the ones that should have plenty of money and more than enough.

The Bible says a lot about economics. The Gospel will EXCITE you. It will make you rich if you OBEY it. If taken seriously, the WORD will make YOU a real *SUCCESS IN FINANCES*. Not only does God love YOU, but He also desires for you to "have more than enough".

All of us are on Divine Assignment on this planet. The Commander-in-Chief of the Universe (Jesus) has given us a mission. Our mission...if we choose to accept it...is to establish His covenant. YOU are a Soldier in His Army filled with the dynamic ability of God. You can make a difference in your community, especially in the area of finances!

CHAPTER 1
The Secret to Success in Finances

What is the secret? One of our missions in life is to tear down the works of satan and be a true Success on this earth. We do not have to be poor or just barely getting by. Greater is Jesus that is in us than all the works on this earth! YOU have the power to loose your finances (Mt.18:18). The WEALTH of God is yours. It belongs to you…His child. God has already given it to you! Reach out and receive it today.

"The blessing of the Lord makes YOU RICH and He adds no sorrow with it" (Literal version of Pr.10:22). Money and riches, when given to you by the Lord, do NOT cause grief, sorrow, suffering, or trouble. God's gifts are holy and pure! His riches bring blessings…NOT grief or sorrow. Sin brings sorrow and…not God's blessings of finances!

Someone once said, "Well, if I were rich with a lot of money, I would probably go back into sin!" The only thing is…there is no Scripture for this fable. What does the Word say? The Word says that God will add no sorrow with His riches that He bestows upon you! His wealth is pure and holy. We should desire it because He wants us to have it! It is His good pleasure to give you the Kingdom.

In the past forty years, I have learned that Christians should be the examples of God's blessings and abundance. After all, we have the "mind of Christ" and KNOW what to do with His gifts and resources! The world does NOT know how to use money or wealth. They have wasted it for thousands of years!

This book hopefully, will give you a balanced and Biblical approach to financial success based upon God's Word. I believe you will develop a keen awareness of God's laws pertaining to finances and your authority

(POWER) to become financially blessed. Understanding these principles will assist you in your ABILITY of becoming an extraordinary winner in today's world. YOU will become a tremendous asset in the Kingdom of God and become a POWERFUL threat to the kingdom of darkness. You are not here by chance, but by the Divine appointment of the Holy Spirit. God will impart His knowledge and wisdom to you as you receive it and use it. His Word is final.

What is the secret? God has made YOU. You are a part of the Family of God. You have Divine purpose. God wants you to be successful, happy, and productive. The GREATEST insurance in the entire world is to get hooked up with Jesus. When He is your Senior Partner, YOU cannot fail. The stock market may crash, wars may rage, famines may come, recessions may appear, and crises may assail, but YOU will NOT fail as you ride with HIM. His Blood Covenant guarantees the very BEST for YOU. Not only do YOU have "fire insurance", but YOU also have recession and depression insurance while on this earth with at least a 30, 60, or hundred-fold return.

Joy, love, peace, contentment, health, abundance, money, and success are yours through the anointing of the Holy Spirit. Expect GOOD things to happen to you and they will. Abundance belongs to you. God is extravagant, but not wasteful. We walk in the Presence of an extraordinary EXTRAVAGANT Father. He loves us so much. He sent us His only begotten Son—Jesus Christ. God was so extravagant that He spared not His only Son. Now, you can begin to walk in His extravagance and enjoy PLENTY (more than enough) because Jesus has already paid for everything. NOW, it is up to us to possess it! Who says there are no more "free rides"? What Jesus did for us is free for the asking! The title deed is ours.

Always reject the limitation complex (sometimes known as the grasshopper complex). Walk in the God-Complex. Be God-conscious and NOT sin-conscious. See yourself as God sees you…a powerful, talented, gifted, and wealthy child of the MOST HIGH.

This beautiful green earth and all of its resources were made for us to ENJOY. God made this earth a paradise for us. God created all the gold, silver, diamonds, and wealth for His children. We are His children. We are the WINNERS. Winners come in first, NOT second. There is no such thing as a good loser. If you are a loser, you are a LOSER and there is nothing good about it. Show me a good loser and I'll show you a defeated person! We do not have to settle for second best.

Our Father has given us a First Class Ticket with all the trimmings. We NOW go forth in power, influence, prestige, money and dignity. The world is saying, "These men and women have been with Jesus." Total success is ours.

Godly success brings greatness into your life because YOU were created for GREATNESS. YOU were created for abundant living. YOU need not lack because the Good Shepherd takes excellent care of you. He lives in your house. And no bank or financial institution can take your house (home) until they evict HIM. As long as He is living there as your Guest, no one can take that dwelling from YOU! Thank God! You are NEVER alone! YOU are safe! YOU are financially solvent with resources to spare. You are healed in His Name (Jesus). You are NOT defeated! ALL THE RESOURCES OF HEAVEN ARE AT YOUR DISPOSAL! God has given YOU true SUCCESS! You do not have to lack another day in Him!

Our Father says, "If you be willing and obedient, you shall eat the good of the land (YOU shall be RICH)" (Is.1:19). Our loving and caring Father loves us! He will NEVER withhold any GOOD thing (resources) from us...EVER. His 32,000 promises are yes and AMEN! He is extremely EXTRAVAGANT! One promise...eternal life would have been enough, but not with Him. He wants us riding in high cotton. He wants us in clover up to our elbows. He wants us to soar with eagles!

Jesus has made us FREE from financial poverty. We are FREE from failure. We are FREE from fear (false effects appearing real). We are FREE from doubt. We are FREE from weakness...defeat...ignorance, sin, lack, bondage, condemnation! WE ARE FREE! Period! Christ paid our debt. He suffered death for two purposes...to set mankind free and to DESTROY the devil who HAD the power of death (Heb.2:14-15). Today, we have incredible POWER (Lk.10:19, 1 Jn.4:17).

Was Jesus poor? Think about it. Was He poor? No! Jesus did have humble beginnings, but this is what the Word says, "...Though He was RICH, yet for your sakes He became poor, that you through His poverty might be RICH (increased in goods, made wealthy, to have abundance such as money)" (2 Cor.8:9). Jesus came to make us rich! This is what this Scripture says! Jesus was a tremendous Success while He was on this earth. He was NOT POOR! He was in heaven with the Father enjoying His heavenly wealth. But the Bible says that He (for our welfare) became poor (for only a short time) that we might be RICH!

Even while Jesus was on this earth, He fed multitudes (thousands) and even had plenty left over. Have you ever fed 5000 men (and their wives and children) at one setting? Or 4000 men (and their wives and children) at another setting? He had a full time treasurer. They had so much MONEY until the treasurer was stealing from Him. They had so much until Jesus commanded Peter to go pay their taxes. Yes, even Jesus had to pay taxes! If Jesus was so poor, why did He pay taxes and talk so much about MONEY?

Now, it is our turn to do some extraordinary things. He has given us His Name and Power to do the same things that He did. All POWER has been given to us (Mt.28:18-19, Lk.10:19) and that includes the POWER to appropriate money and resources and get wealth (Deut.8:18). We have no excuse for being POOR...NONE. I know that Jesus said..."that we would always have the poor with us". Why? Because they have not acted on God's Word about success in finances. We also will have sinners on this earth until Jesus comes. Do they have to remain sinners? No! Do people have to remain poor? No!

Some Christians are always talking about "when we get to heaven, we will be rich". Of course, you will be wealthy in heaven, but God also wants us to have abundance, more than enough NOW. He has already given it to us. We need to reach out and possess it.

BOTTOMLINE: The secret to *Success in Finances* is to know that our Father God wants us to be rich because we are His children. Over 800 Scriptures in the Bible are about finances. His resources are ours for the taking. We must tear down the strongholds of poverty. We must refuse the enemy any foothold in our finances. We do not have to put up with the devil's evil schemes and devices. He has no power over our finances except the power that we give to him. Let us choose to give him NONE.

CHAPTER 2
Money…Sweet Money

What do you think about money? Do you have more than enough? Enough to give to God's purposes and others? The way you feel and think about money will determine how much \$\$\$ you accumulate. Your attitude toward money affects your finances, thought processes, emotions, and your passion. "Money is the answer for everything" (Eccl. 10:19).

Do you have enough money? Do you have more than enough? Can you believe this? "And the people continued to bring freewill offerings morning after morning. So all the skilled craftsmen who were doing all the work on the sanctuary left their work and said to Moses, "The people are bringing more than enough for doing the work the LORD commanded to be done. Then Moses gave an order and they sent this word throughout the camp: "No man or woman is to give anything else as an offering for the sanctuary." And so the people were restrained from bringing more, because what they already had more than enough to do all the work" (Ex.36:3-7).

The people GAVE to God!

Many people do not have enough \$\$\$. When you have enough money, you don't think about it very often. But when you have too little, you think about it all the time. What is your attitude toward \$\$\$. Your attitude toward \$\$\$ depends on how much money you have. Some people feel they have too little \$\$\$. Some people feel they have more than enough.

Arguments over money are a major reason for divorce. Problems with money are the primary reason for business failure. Sometimes, the wrong attitude toward money may cause sickness. It's not uncommon for people to even kill themselves over money problems.

We must deal with life as it is…not as we wish it were or could be. Some people live in a world of self-delusion with regard to money. They wish, hope, and pray about $$$…while at the same time, they are thinking and saying, "My dreams will never materialize". Remember, wealthy people are no different from you and me. They just "know more" about money matters.

What is the secret? Knowledge is power. Knowing more about $$$ can mean more earning power. One of the most common obstacles to achieving financial independence is the belief that somehow money is wrong and that people who have a lot of it are evil. This belief is not based on facts.

Money is good! It takes money to buy homes, churches, cars, clothes, food, and the good things in life. Money has energy. It is largely attracted to people who treat it well. Money tends to flow toward those who can use it in the most productive ways in giving and benefiting others. Money flows away from those who use it poorly or who refuse to give to God's purposes!

Your attitude toward money that can affect your quality of life. Be perfectly honest with yourself about money…Pretending that you don't care about money will only make you unhappy. Think about all the wonderful things that you could have in your life if you had more $$$. Then, think of all the things that you could do to increase the amount you earn and the amount you keep. How can you attract more wealth and the abundance life? Wealth is everywhere. The real question is how do you gain this abundance…more than enough?

Why are some people more successful than others? You are where you are and what you are because of "you"…not someone else. Everything you are today or ever will be is up to you. Your life today is the result of your choices, decisions, and actions. You can create a positive future by changing your behavior. You can make new choices and decisions that are more consistent with the real you and what you want to be. What you are or will be…is up to you. The only limit on what you can be is up to your own imagination. Take control of your destiny by taking complete control of your thoughts, words, actions, and $$$.

What is success in regards to $$$? I believe it is the ability to live your life the way you want to live it…doing what you enjoy…surrounded by people who you admire and respect. It is the ability to achieve your dreams, desires, hopes, aspirations, wishes, and goals. Each of us is unique, but we all have four basic goals and desires:

- We want to stay healthy with a high level of energy.
- We want to enjoy excellent relationships…intimate, personal, and social…with the people we love and respect.
- We want to do work which we enjoy and do it well and get paid well for it.
- We want to achieve financial independence. We want to reach the point in life where we have more than enough money so that we never have to worry about money again. We want to be completely free of financial worries.
- THE KEY: Give a portion to God and to others!

Now days, we hear a lot about money. Contrary to what some may say, money is not the root of all evil. Money is neutral. It does what we tell it to do. It buys what we tell it to buy. We can spend it for good or for evil. The choice is ours. The Bible says that the "love of money is the root of all evil", not money. Because you are a special creation of God, YOU can have MONEY and great SUCCESS at the same time! YOU have all the POWER in the universe wrapped up within YOU right now to assist you in this venture. You have God the Father living within you. You have Jesus Christ abiding within you. You have the Holy Spirit living within you! What other power do you need? You now have the power to take control of your life and finances. YOU can pull down the strongholds or cast down anything that would exalt itself against your finances (2 Cor.10:4-5). Why? Because YOU are made in the direct image of God. Is God poor? Or is God WEALTHY? Success and money are YOURS!

In the Kingdom of God, it is true that there are many things better than money, such as the Word of God, your good name, your wonderful spouse, your children, your eternal soul, the anointing of the Holy Spirit upon your life, and the precious BLOOD of JESUS. These blessings cannot be purchased with money. It is self evident that money is not the most important thing in Scripture. However, the bottom-line is this: It takes money to propagate the world with the Gospel and proclaim the good news of eternal life to this sinful and dying generation. It takes money to pay our just and honest debts. It takes money for our education, homes, automobiles, clothes, food, and other important needs. It takes money to build churches in America and other nations. Money can answer a lot of needs on this earth (Eccl. 10:19).

God has given you dominion (the right and power to govern and control) over everything that creeps, crawls, swims, flies, or walks (Gen.1:28). You have the POWER and RIGHT to govern and control your financial circumstances. YOU have the ability to make money. God has made you able.

Jesus said, "Behold, I give unto YOU power (authority) over ALL the power of the enemy: and nothing (not one little or big thing) shall by any means hurt YOU" (Lk.10:19). Authority means the right to exercise power. You have the right to take authority over your finances! God's resources and money belong to YOU!

"...They marveled and glorified God, which had given such power (delegated authority) unto men" (Mt.9:8). Jesus had the right to use the full power of attorney of God. He acted in the Father's stead. He took His Divine orders from His Father God. He did the will of the Father. He and God were One. They thought alike. God thought it and Jesus did it! Today, you have the same right. You are a son/daughter of God. You deserve to have money...PLENTY of it...more than enough. Poverty does not belong to a king! Money belongs to kings!

Jesus said, "And I will give unto YOU the keys (power and authority) of the kingdom..." (Mt.16:19). These were the keys of the kingdom which gave us all power and authority, even to make money. They also gave us the abilities of binding and loosing (Mt.18:18). These KEYS will work miracles in your FINANCES!

Again, Jesus said, "...ALL power (and authority) is given unto Me in heaven and in earth. (YOU) go therefore..." (Mt.28: 18-19). How do we go? We go as winners in the area of finances; we go in His power and authority. The Bible gives us the power and authority we need through the finished work of Jesus Christ. "…As He (Jesus) is (present tense), so are we (YOU and I) in this world" (1 Jn.4:17). Is Jesus poor NOW?

Many Christians have formed the opinion that God is against His children having material wealth for fear that they would lose their souls. However, the Bible is full of accounts of God blessing men/women with prosperity (Gen.13:3-9, 26:12; 1 Kgs.10:29; Job 1:3; Ps.35:27). God has promised in the Old and New Testaments…riches and blessings untold to those who will serve and obey Him (Deut.28:1-15, 29:9; Josh.1:7-9; 2 Cor.8:9, 9:6-11). God Himself is the richest Person in the universe…So if it is a sin to be rich, then He is the greatest sinner of all. Of course, we know that God is NOT a sinner. He is the Most Righteous One of the universe! In Heaven, the streets are paved with gold. The foundation is garnished with all kinds of jewels. Every house is a mansion and the gates are solid pearls! If God has promised us these things in the next life, why would it be a sin to have some of these things now in this present life?

Wall Street, NASDAC, and the National Treasury spend billions of dollars proving that…"Security" is elusive at best, absent on most occasions and limited more often than desired. However, we do not need to fear! In our fast-paced society today, many well intentioned individuals often fall prey and victim to fear and failure…in the area of finances because…"Their gage of security was the provision and not the Provider." Only Jehovah Jireh is our every Provider. God has a principle of economic security that cannot fail. It is called "FAITH". What does faith have to do with it?

Faith, the one-word formula of confidence allows us to trust in God for our well-being, especially in finances. The Bible is actually a historical account of how faithful God is to those who live by faith. Faith is "knowing that God is able" before we pray…and then maintaining that He is able…Until the fruition and completion of the partition. In the seasons of life when His abundance overtakes us, faith still means that He is our Provider.

"But You shall receive power (inherent power and ability) after that the Holy Ghost is come upon YOU…" (Acts 1:8). God has given you His power and ability and strength. He has given you the best He has to offer. USE it and become a resourceful BELIEVER in His Kingdom! Use it and make a lot of money…big money! Greater is the wealth that is in YOU than the poverty that is in the world. You have more riches within YOU than you will ever need or use. To make or have money, you must have faith in God! Doubt will steal you blind! Doubt will kill you financially. Doubt will create bills when there are none. Doubt will wipe out a whole family financially. Doubt is a KILLER. In Caleb's day, doubt wiped out a whole generation of wealthy people (hundreds of thousands) and their bodies fell dead in the wilderness (Nu.14: 29). They had money, but they allowed the enemy to steal it from them…and rip them off!

We must take our eyes off the problem. We must quit speaking the problem. We must not speak lack. Remember Caleb? He was a GIANT of a man in faith. Even though doubt was all around, he did not speak it. He spoke of "an EXCEEDING good land…flowing with milk and honey. The people are bread for us. Their defense is gone. The Lord is with us…fear them not. They are only wimps. Their money is ours for the taking" (Author's version Nu. 14:7-9).

What ever happened to Caleb? Payday came to his house! God promised General Caleb and his children the very land that he had trodden upon when he had spied out the land (De.1:36). As a big SUCCESS in finances, Caleb was not shy. To have money in today's world, you cannot afford to be shy. The spirit of timidity is not of God. YOU must be BOLD. Caleb reminded Joshua that he had "WHOLLY followed the Lord" (Jos.14:8) and he wanted what was coming to him. Caleb wanted his MOUNTAIN of finances. It was payday! Joshua blessed Caleb and gave him the mountain that had been promised to him. This particular payday was also Caleb's birthday (85 years old). WHAT A PRESENT! General Caleb had certainly earned it. At last he could go in and enjoy his success in finances! Caleb had faith! No devil or giant was going to rob or steal it from him. He had a made up mind to succeed. Our minds must be made up! Do YOU want to succeed in finances? If the answer is YES, then YOU shall!

In short, although we have been given everything in this life to put us over, we still must go in and possess our money. Christ has equipped us with gifts, spiritual weapons, wisdom, warfare plans (Bible), and POWER through the Holy Ghost. He has commissioned us to go forth and use His POWER to be successes in finances! Money belongs to us! But we must PRESS OUR WAY IN! Poverty has to bow at the Name of Jesus. Our bills will be paid in the mighty Name of Jesus. We are MIGHTY conquerors, not the conquered. We are the MIGHTY victors, not the victims. Poverty is not our master. We master poverty by rendering it powerless and paralyzed in the Name of Jesus.

Get ready. Get EXCITED. You are God's success for this generation. You are a winner. You are equipped with God's power, authority, ability, prosperity, and anointing. God watches over His Word to perform it and make it happen. No devil, fool, imp, demon, or person can stop the 32,000 promises of God. You are a WINNER! God is FOR you. He is on your side. You are the VICTOR! You cannot go under for going OVER!" You deserve the very best that God has to offer. The LORD will make sure that you have MONEY because you belong to His Family. Go out now and use the power and authority that He has given to you to get WEALTH. You will NOT fail in Jesus' Name.

CHAPTER 3
As a Man Thinks

Another secret…You are what you think about. You become what you think about. If you think lack, you will have plenty of it. Success is determined by what you think. 95% of everything that you think, feel, do, and achieve is the result of your thinking….and habits. Beginning in childhood, you developed a series of conditioned responses that lead you to react automatically without thinking in almost every situation.

Successful people think success. Unsuccessful people do not. Successful, happy, and prosperous men and women…say the right things in the right way…and normally at the right time. As a result, they accomplish ten to twenty times as much as the average person. Why? Their thinking habits and behaviors…Therefore, success is the ability to achieve your dreams and desires.

Think about this for a moment. Currently, what do you think about when you think of Wall Street? Do you actually think about stocks and bonds? Probably not…If you're like most people, you have one thing on your mind when thinking about the economy…MONEY! That's right. You can try to skirt the real issue, but it all comes back to money. If you have stocks, bonds, certificates, 401Ks, etc, you are thinking "MONEY". Some will always say, "Well, money is not everything." And that is a true statement. Money is not everything; however, without it, you will not have anything. So, let's get real…We all need money to pay our mortgages, credit card bills, and utilities. We need to buy groceries, gasoline, clothes, shoes, and give to God, especially our local Church… and to other charities.

How do you go from rags to riches in one generation? Isaac did. "Now there was a famine in the land…Isaac planted crops in that land

and the SAME YEAR reaped a hundredfold because the LORD blessed him. The man became rich, very rich…and his wealth continued to grow until he became very wealthy. He had so many flocks, herds, and servants that the Philistines envied him" (Gen.26). Isaac thought success.

How did I go from rags to riches? I was reared in the poorest town in the poorest county in the State of Florida. I was so poor, I couldn't even pay attention. I came from a family of nine. We went to town once a week. Sometimes, my father would buy me an ice-cream bar or a Coke. Many times, I had to put card-board in my shoes to cover up the holes in the soles of my shoes. I would still get sand in my shoes though. Often, I would wear hand-me-down clothes. My first bicycle was a used Western Flyer…painted dark blue. I used it for my paper route. We played stick ball for entertainment. When I was in the second grade, I had a total of two shirts…and a pair of worn out shoes. I was poor, but didn't know it. Poverty is a curse, not a Christian virtue.

One day the preacher preached on tithing. I listened to what he said. My first tithe was 35 cents. I felt good paying tithes. That was the day that I began to prosper and have monumental success in my life. Even though I was still poor, I didn't feel poor anymore. I had God's promise. "Bring all the tithes into the storehouse…That there may be food in My house, And try Me now in this," Says the LORD of hosts, "If I will not open for you the windows (FLOODGATES) of heaven And pour out for you such a blessing That there will not be room enough to receive it" (Mal.3).

I began to stake my entire financial life and success on this one Scripture. For 54 years, it has worked for me…and continues to work. Today, I have "more than enough". God does not lie. I have talked to thousands…either in person, radio, TV, or through my books about the "Law of Tithing and Giving". By the way some people who do not give… think that God lied when He said that He would bless us as we pay our tithes and give in offerings.

Think about Who God is. He is not some Rock Star making a lot of noise. He is not a movie actor. He is not some worldly celebrity or Pop Idol. He is not some politician making promises that will be broken. He is the Commander-in-Chief of the Universe. He is Jehovah-Jireh. He is God! God Himself was speaking in Mal.3:10-12. When God speaks, we should listen, especially when He is talking about MONEY.

Giving to God will help us to achieve our most important goals. Tithing will assist us in achieving success. Our character will grow and our wisdom will increase in financial maturity. We will become the kind of person that others look up to and admire. Givers become leaders in our communities.

I am NOT a self-made man. I had to get rid of self in the area of finances in order to obey God in giving. Everything I have, I owe to God. He is the One Who made it happen for me with more than enough.

You came into this world with the most incredible brain...surrounded by unlimited possibilities for success, happiness, and achievement. You even have a manufacturer's handbook...called the Bible. With God's help, you can figure out most money matters. However, without His help, life can be most difficult, especially with a lot of debt...If you are going to tear down strongholds and level to the ground the ambushes of satan that he has placed against your finances, then you MUST be armed with the Word of God concerning finances, especially "tithing". *Success in Finances* dictates that you should study the Word regularly on prosperity. You will then be knowledgeable and well versed about what God says concerning money. You should also KNOW the blessings of TITHING.

I know that some Christians do not believe in tithing! They need the Word of God. They need instruction from God's Word. Some think that it is unnecessary to pay tithes. This type of thinking will bring about a desert...a desert of dearth...a desert of lack...a desert of famine in a person's life.

To be successful in money matters, we have to learn the true value of tithing! I have learned to STAND on my OWN TWO FEET and give up no ground when it comes to tithing. Give up nothing! Do not compromise! Be tenacious and persistent. Give up no ground. Never compromise on the issue of tithing. Tithing means giving ten percent of your income to God. It is not 20 percent, 30 percent, or 50 percent. It is simply 10 percent! Whatever else you give beyond the 10 percent is simply offerings. And oh by the way, your tithes belong to your local church…no exceptions! I find no Scripture that gives you permission to pay your tithes to some other ministry…other than where you worship locally. It is called the "storehouse". Oh, I know all the excuses, but they have no merit when it comes to Scripture!

The enemy has NO power today over your tithes. As a matter of fact, he has NO power over you at all. He is NOT alive and well as some may think. The devil can only roar as a lion. He is not a lion. The true Lion of Judah is Jesus Christ. If power could be equated to gasoline, he would not have enough for a red ant's motorcycle to drive around a BB. The only power he has is the power that we give to him. Let us choose to give him NONE!

As a prosperous Christian, you need to pay your tithes. If you fail to pay your tithes, you will be walking under a curse. You will be headed straight for financial disaster. Poverty will be your self-made, man-made cross…which has nothing to do with God. When you fail to pay tithes, your financial door is WIDE open for the enemy to play havoc with your money and success!

You must DECIDE…DECREE…and DECLARE (Job 22:28) that the first 10 percent of your income will go to God as your tithe:

1. Make that decision. Determine that you are going to pay your tithe. DECIDE to pay your tithe.

2. Decree it (Ps.2:7). Decree means to appoint, note, print, set, to order, ordain, command, or establish. DECREE to pay your tithe.

3. Declare it. Declare in the Hebrew means "to dig, as one would dig a well." Declaring is like digging a well. If you dig long enough and deep enough, you will get water, oil, or gas. RESOURCES will come as you pay your tithe. DECLARE that YOU WILL pay your tithe!

As a tithe payer, you must have enthusiasm which means in the Greek: in God violently involved. Tithing must become a lifestyle with you. Remember, that 10 percent of your paycheck is God's money, not yours. If you spend God's money, you are not wise. People who rob God are LOSERS! They seldom prosper! Payday for them will come someday… and it will not be a good payday!

Abraham paid tithes 430 years before the law of Moses (Gen.14:20). Jacob said, "…I will surely give the tenth" (Gen.28:22). The Leviticus law said, "ALL THE TITHE BELONGS TO THE LORD…IT IS HOLY UNTO THE LORD" (Lev.27:30).

In the New Testament, Christ taught Tithing (Mt.23:23, Lk.18:11-12, 42; Mt. 5:20, Lk.10:7). Read these Scriptures in the Living Bible.

The Book of Hebrews taught tithing (7:1-8).

Paul taught tithing (1Tim.5:18, 1 Cor. 9:14, Gal.6:6).

Tithing is NOT optional. I have heard some Christians say, "Well, tithing is optional". This is NOT scriptural. Tithing is NOT optional! Period! It is necessary for EVERY child of God. The TITHE (1/10) BELONGS TO GOD. He gave us 9/10's to live on. If we become greedy and spend HIS money, we will be stealing and will place ourselves back under the curse. Being under the curse is non-productive, reckless, and irresponsible.

Tithing and giving brings wealth to the GODLY (Ps. 112). Tithing is only part of the equation. The other part is giving above your tithe. Tithing opens the door and giving is the icing on the cake. In Malachi 3, God talks about tithes and offerings. If you do both, the LORD says that He will open up the windows of heaven, and pour you out a blessing… that there shall not be room enough to receive.

Tommy Franks says, "Paying tithes is not enough to be successful in money matters and Biblical Economics." The other side of the coin is "offerings". Many saints are tithing, but have empty pockets, empty wallets, and empty purses. Why? Because they do not understand that tithing only opens the windows of heaven. It does not determine the 30/60/100 fold return. Our offerings do...not the tithe. The tithe already belongs to God. It is not ours. It belongs to God! He allows us to determine our offerings, not our tithe. The more generous our offerings (seed), greater will be the harvest.

As we pay our tithe, things will begin to happen. YOU see, as we stand in the Father's presence without the sense of guilt or inferiority, we will begin to be conscious of success...conscious of God, His Son, the Holy Spirit, faith, and love. Locked up in each of us (the inner man, 1 Pet. 3:4) is the ABILTIY of GOD to make money. You will begin to have faith in your own faith as you believe the Word of God on tithing. As you are obedient in tithing, YOU will have His ability and wealth. You will have His wisdom. You will have His love. You will have His righteousness (1 Cor. 1:30).

What does tithing have to do with it? God loves us so much! As we are OBEDIENT to the Word, the following will begin to take place in our lives:

- We can run through a troop (Ps. 18:29).
- We can leap over a wall (Ps. 18:29).
- We can chase a thousand (Deut. 32:30).
- Two can chase 10,000 (Jos. 23:10).
- Your enemies shall flee before you SEVEN ways (Deut.28:7).
- God has declared that we are his CHILDREN (Jn.1:12).

Jesus came to destroy the works of the devil (1 Jn.3:8). He has made you the head and not the tail (Deut.28:13). Upon the return of Christ some day, He will set up His own global system of finances. He will have a BALANCED BUDGET.

We have what we think and say. We never rise above our confession. Even in the first chapter of Genesis, the words "God said" were stated ten times. Scripturally, God has never done anything without first speaking it into existence. And God said, Let there be light and there was light.

"God said, Let there be a firmament in the midst of the waters. God said, Let the earth bring forth grass…and fruit trees yielding fruit after their kind…and it was so. God said, Let there be lights in the firmament. God said, Let the land produce living creatures according to their kinds. God said, Let us make man in our image."

"For verily I SAY unto you, that whosoever shall SAY unto this mountain, Be thou removed, and be thou cast into the sea; and shall not doubt in his heart, but shall believe that those things which he SAYS shall come to pass; he shall have whatsoever he SAYS" (Mk.11:23). GOD is for US. GOD is on OUR SIDE. GOD wants

US to PROSPER and be SUCCESSFUL.

CHAPTER 4
Success in the Law of Giving

For the past three years Karen and I have attended the church that George Washington, George Mason, and George Fairfax built in 1774. What a privilege it was to sit in the pew that belonged to him. George Washington is often called "The Father of Our Country." He was admired for the quality of his character and his behavior. But that is not the way George Washington started off in life. He came from a middle class family with few advantages. As a young man aspiring to succeed and prosper, he came across a little book entitled "The Rules of Civility and Decent Behavior in Company and Conversation." As a teenage boy, he copied those 110 rules into a personal notebook. He carried it with him and reviewed them constantly throughout his life. By practicing the "Rules of Civility," he developed his habits, behavior, and manners. He learned successful habits and made a lot of money.

Benjamin Franklin, who began as a printer's apprentice went on to become the first self-made millionaire in America. His secret: He worked on his personality to develop virtue, temperance, tolerance, and tranquility. He eventually became one of the most popular personalities and statesmen in America. He became influential in Paris as an Ambassador. He was a tremendous asset during the Revolutionary War and the Constitutional Convention. By working on himself and his habits, he shaped history. He too, made a lot of money.

Only you and God are in complete control of your destiny and earning potential. With God's help, you can fulfill your destiny. You are an extraordinary person! You came into this world with more talents and abilities than you can ever use. You can not exhaust your full potential if you lived 100 lifetimes. Your brain has 20 billion cells…each of which is connected to 20 thousand other cells. The possible combinations and arrangement of ideas, thoughts, and insights that you can generate are unlimited. Your final destination (Heaven) was prepared for YOU from the foundation of the world. It's the Father's GOOD pleasure to give you the kingdom.

You are wonderfully and fearfully made. God knows you, your ways, your thoughts, your words, and every hair on your head. God made you special! He formed your inward parts while you were still in your mother's womb. God fashioned you, designed you, appointed you, and brought you into this world. You are marvelously and incredibly made. You are the ONLY you. You are made of water, fluid, calcium, iron, carbon, lime, fiber, and other tissues. You have 263 bones, 970 miles of blood vessels, and 20,000 hairs in your ears alone. You have 10 million nerves and nerve endings, 600 million air cells in your lungs. Your heart beats 4200 times an hour and pumps 24,000 pounds of blood every 24 Hours.

Even when you were only an embryo, you were on the mind of God. You are the "apple" of His eye. You are the BEST product that heaven ever produced. According to Scripture, God has even written a book about you which contains all the days of your life. God planned each of your days before you were born. You are very special to Him! Whatever you have accomplished in life up to this point…is only a small fraction of what you are truly capable of achieving.

Abraham Maslow (psychologist) once wrote, "The story of the human race is the story of men and women selling themselves far too short." The average person settles for "far less" than he/she is truly capable of achieving. Compared with what you could be, everything you have accomplished thus far is only a small part of what is truly possible for you.

I started off in life with no advantages. My father was a carpenter…a good one, but not enough income for nine people. Sometimes, he would be unemployed between jobs. We never seemed to have enough money. I began working at the age of eight…paying for my own clothes and expenses. I mowed lawns…had a paper route…and other odd jobs.

As a teenager, I remember one time going to bed in the middle of the afternoon crying my eyes out because I did not have a job…and did not have any money to buy new shoes. My one and only pair of shoes were worn out. I cried for a long time.

I believe everything happens for a reason. Nothing happens by accident. This experience caused me to realize that poverty is a curse and not a virtue. At that point, I made a determination in my spirit, soul, and mind that one day I would have "more than enough".

How did I get out of poverty? I began to give my way out. I also started to read every Scripture in the Bible on the topic of money and wealth. I looked at the successful men and women in the Bible. I looked at their habits, especially Joseph's. I realized that God has no respect of persons. If He did it for Joseph, Abraham, Isaac, and Jacob, He would do it for me...no exception. Money belongs to the children of God who give to God. Giving to God is the greatest key (not secret) to accumulating money and wealth. It is not a matter of luck, chance, or accident. The Law of Success is found in Scripture.

The price for our prosperity, joy, self-esteem, healing, and forgiveness of sins has been paid in full. Jesus paid our bills in full. Jesus was a Giver. We are also givers. Givers never lose. Selfishness never wins!

A successful person does more than just talk. He also demonstrates his actions through love...and love always means giving. YOU as a Believer are guaranteed SUCCESS in Life if YOU do the following:

1. BELIEVE that it is God's will for you to prosper (3 Jn 2, Prov. 13:22, Deut. 8:18, Ps. 112).

2. Make God your SENIOR PARTNER (Ps. 37:3-6, Isa. 58:14, MT. 6:33, Jn. 10:10).

3. DREAM...DREAM...DREAM. NEVER STOP DREAMING. Have a VISION. Think BIG. Dream BIG. Think ABUNDANCE (Joel 2:28, Acts 2:17, Gen. 37:5, 1 Kg. 3:5, 18:41; 2 Cor.12:1, Prov. 29:18).

4. Recognize God as the SOURCE of YOUR Supply (Lk.6:38, Deut. 8:18, Prov. 10:22, 2 Pet. 1:3, Ps. 75:6-7, Isa. 48:17-18, Ps. 1:3).

5. You do not have to lack (Mt. 11:12, Gen. 1:26-28, Ps. 8:4-9, Heb. 2:6-16, Eph. 1:22).

6. GIVE…GIVE…GIVE (Lk. 6:38, Prov. 3:9-10, 2 Cor. 8:7). You MUST be a giver in order to have lasting and true success in finances.

7. Begin to think big. You are God's very own child made IN HIS IMAGE (Ps. 82:6, Jn. 10:34-36, Eph. 5:30).

8. GET READY for His Blessings (Job 27:16-17, Prov. 28:8, Eccl. 2:26, Jn. 8:32, Deut. 8:18, Isa. 61:6, Eccl. 6:1-2). As you become a systematic giver, success will come to you and your house.

The Laws of God are for our welfare. The law of giving is absolute. "For the law of the Spirit of Life in Christ Jesus has freed me from the law of sin and death" (Amp. Rom. 8:2).

These writings are not an in-depth or exhaustive study on the law of giving or *Success in Finances* due to the time element involved; however, if you will use these principles as a springboard, YOU will HAVE a solid foundation for future studies and research on these topics. My thoughts and concepts will serve only as instruments and tools to assist you in studying the WORD and finances for YOURSELF.

Jesus said to give (Lk. 6:38). He said to give first. THEN…"it shall be given unto you Good (beautiful, valuable, honest, worthy, virtuous) MEASURE." Measure means: quantity, degree, proportion. Jesus said the measure would be "Pressed down, shaken together, RUNNING OVER (above, beyond, to overflow, exceeding abundantly, to GUSH out as a belly gusher)."

Do you KNOW what Jesus was actually saying? "If you give, you will receive! Your gift will return to you in full and overflowing measure, pressed down, shaken together to make room for more, and running over. Whatever measure you use to give-large or small-will be used to measure what is given back to you" (Living Bible).

If you give a teaspoon full, you will get the reward of a teaspoon back to you. If you give a coffee can full, you will be rewarded back a coffee can full…or bucket…wheelbarrow…dump truck…drag line…or a box car full. If you sow abundantly, you will reap abundantly! Of the 35 parables found in the gospels in which Christ taught, more than a third deal either directly or indirectly with money or the law of giving.

I remember in 1971 when I was bankrupt in every area of my life. I did not have two nickels to rub together. I didn't have a job. I was a loser…a broke loser. They even came and repossessed my car. At that time in my life, I decided to file for bankruptcy; however, I did not have the $50 filing fee. I was so poor until I could not even file for bankruptcy. My life was in shambles. I owed thousands of dollars and I was penniless. I got angry at the devil for stealing from me. But I was ignorant of the Word, so I did not know how to combat the enemy. Most Christians that I knew at that time did not know either. So I got ANGRY at the devil.

I was sick and tired of LOSING. I cried and wept, but to no avail. Things just got worse. What was I to do? Finally, one day as I was soul searching and praying, the Lord spoke to me. He said, "Tommy, you can get out of debt." I opened my eyes. I looked around. I knew it was God speaking to me. I responded, "But God, how?"

This time it was as clear as a bell. He said, "Give your way out." I felt like asking, "Is there someone else up there?" I mean…I had nothing to give or at least it seemed that way. The devil will oftentimes tell you that you have nothing to give. God always says to give what you have. If an offering plate passes before you, GIVE SOMETHING, even if it is only your spare change. I am SERIOUS! Never let an offering plate pass before you without giving something.

Anyway, that was all that the Lord said to me that day about finances. I began to search the Scriptures on finances. When I got to Malachi 3:8-9, I immediately saw my financial problem. I had been wayward. I had not been paying my tithes like I should. Each time I failed to pay tithes, I was stealing from God. I felt like a thief and a robber. I asked God for forgiveness and began to give…sometimes, it was small. But I gave whenever the offering plate was passed. I began to pay my tithe and give in offerings. It takes both to prosper…TITHING and OFFERINGS!

Let me repeat that. It takes both tithing and offerings to prosper. As previously stated, some saints of God are tithing in accordance with the Scriptures found in Malachi 3:8-10, but still have empty pockets. It is called open windows with empty pockets. "Will a man rob God? Yet ye have robbed me. But you say, Wherein have we robbed You? In tithes AND offerings." The tithe is God's. It is not ours. He allows us to determine our offerings, not our tithe. Tithing opens the windows of heaven. Our offerings determine the measure of God's blessings that flow from those windows back to us…sometimes 30…60…100 fold. Your blessings will be poured out according to the measure you have given.

Let us examine Malachi 3:8-12 a little closer:
- God said to prove (test) Him.
- Then He would open the windows of heaven…
- And pour YOU out a blessing…
- That YOU would not have room enough to receive it.
- ALL nations would call you blessed.
- YOU would be acceptable, favored, and valuable.

Giving is the key! The Lord told Moses that "every man" should give with his heart willingly (Ex.25:2).

In 1972 I began to give every time an offering was taken. In 1975 the Lord told me to triple my offerings. Two years later, He told me to double my giving in offerings again. About three years later, He again told me to increase my offerings some more. As I responded in obedience each time, the Lord added abundantly to my finances. TODAY, I can buy anything I need or desire. Thank God for Jesus and His Word.

Twelve Thousand Israelites fought against the Midianites and won. $30 Million was the booty (spoils of battle). Not one single Israelite was lost in battle. They gave a special thanksgiving offering of $10,000 beyond the $331,580 they had already given (Nu.31:50).

WHO GAVE? Every man…Every man gave. The Word says, "They shall not appear before the Lord EMPTY" (Deut.16:16, Ex.23:15, 34:20). He was not talking about being empty headed. He was talking about empty pocket books…money or gifts.

WHO SHALL GIVE? Every man...How shall he give? As he is able..."And none shall appear before ME Empty." When we give, we need to give our first fruits, not our leftovers (Prov. 3:9-10). Some misguided saints are trying to give God their leftovers and then wondering, "Why the Lord is not blessing them in abundance". God wants His portion right off the TOP.

Some Christians even say that giving was only under the law. I have news for you. The New Testament Scriptures also propagate and command giving. Look at 1 Cor. 16:1-3. WHO was SUPPOSE to GIVE? Everyone...HOW? As God prospered them...

Another scripture found in 2 Cor. 9:7 says EVERY MAN...What happens when we give cheerfully? Acts 4:34 says, "Neither was there any among them that lacked..." Pr. 11:25 says, "The liberal soul shall be made FAT..."

Acts 11:29 says EVERY MAN...according to his ability. He (Jesus) was so very rich, yet He became poor so that you and I could be RICH (2 Cor.8:9). Our Lord is rich unto us (Rom.10:12). RICH means: to be increased in goods, to make wealthy such as $$$, possessions, abundance, and riches.

IT is UNSCRIPTURAL to PRAY for THOSE who "do not have to give in offerings." WHY? Because Jesus said to give and then it would be given unto you. The reason that some people do not have is: They have not given. What does the WORD say? "...that person who does not have, even the little he has shall be taken from him..." (Mt.13:12, Mk.4:25). That really seems harsh to some people, but it is not harsh. God's Word is NOT grievous.

Jesus also bears this principle out when He says, "Give and it shall be given unto you..." (Lk. 6:38). Jesus has never lied and never will. He said that if you would give (something) then you would have more. That's financial success.

What did bold Elijah have to say about Giving FIRST (1 Kings 17:8-16)? Elijah told the widow to make him a cake FIRST! Even though the widow was reluctant about sharing her last meal with the prophet (1 Kgs.17).

- Elijah said to her, "Don't be afraid. Go home and do as you have said. But first make a small cake of bread for me from what you have and bring it to me, and then make something for yourself and your son. For this is what the LORD, the God of Israel, says: 'The jar of flour will not be used up and the jug of oil will not run dry until the day the LORD gives rain on the land.' "She went away and did as Elijah had told her. So there was food every day for Elijah and for the woman and her family. For the jar of flour was not used up and the jug of oil did not run dry, in keeping with the word of the LORD spoken by Elijah."

She gave and then it was given unto her in abundance. Today, in our society the religious ones would back bite Elijah and blame God for not assisting the widow in a timely manner!

If we obey God's Law on Giving, the returns on our deposits will be fantastic. When will we get to enjoy these returns? The Word says, "NOW in this life..." (Mk.10:28-30, Lk. 18:30, Mt.19:29). What type of return will it be? It will be the best in the universe...30/60/100 fold.

When I was just a small child, my father took us to a tent meeting. That night the evangelist was speaking about giving. He said, "Prove God. See what God will do when you give to Him. Give tonight out of your need. He will bless you abundantly."

My father had ten dollars to his name and had been laid off from his job for several days. He also had nine mouths to feed; nonetheless, he obeyed the man of God. He gave his last ten dollars...the only money between his family and starvation. Yet, he obeyed God!

After the service, we all got in the old car and traveled back to Zolfo Springs, Florida. As my father opened the front door of our home, the black telephone was ringing. It was his business agent wanting to know if he would accept another job the next morning. My father was overwhelmed! He immediately said, "Yes, of course, I will." After he hung up the receiver, he praised the Lord and then shared what had happened with us.

That last $10 certainly brought in more than a hundred-fold return. My father made thousands of dollars on that next job. You see, my father was also a carpenter that patterned his life after the carpenter's Son who lived in Nazareth.

Isaac sowed in FAMINE (Gen. 26:1-16). There was a famine in the land of Canaan. God had said, "Do not go down to Egypt…" The Word says that Isaac sowed in famine and received in the same year 100 FOLD. Even the Philistines envied him. You can sow in famine or during your need and reap a harvest the same year. My father sowed $10 out of his need and received over 100 fold the same year! You can too if you obey God and act on His Word.

Have you ever tried to out give God? Have you ever proved Him at His Word on "giving"? I challenge you to do so. Many times in the past, I have given my last dollar. I can even remember borrowing a car, buying gas on credit, driving a good distance, and then speaking at a large church…and not receiving a cent for my teaching of the Gospel! That type of negligence concerned me, but it did NOT steal my joy! Nonetheless, God would always send someone to meet my need. TODAY, friend, He will not only meet your needs, but He will also give you your heart's desire (Ps.37:4, Mk.11:24).

In the summer of 1974, I told the Lord, "I am going to prove you according to Malachi 3:10. I have a particular need that must be paid soon." I told the Lord the amount of money needed to pay the bill. Three days later, I received a phone call from out of state. The voice on the other end said, "Tommy, we have been thinking about sending you some money. As a matter of fact, we are going to send it immediately."

They sent the money. The amount was almost identical (within a few cents) of the amount that I had told the Lord about a few days earlier.

Now, some may say, "Well, if that had been God, it would have been the exact amount." Do not think like a fool. Fools allow the letter of the law to rob and kill them. The Spirit gives life. If I remember correctly, I believe it was more than enough to take care of the bill. And it was sent from another state. If God has to send MONEY ($$$) to you from another country (even Africa), your needs and desires will be met. Thank God for His Word about money! As long as you give according to the Law of Giving, you will abundantly be BLESSED by God the Father, Son, and Holy Spirit.

CHAPTER 5
Money Matters in Finances

What is the secret to The Law of Success? "Give and it shall be given unto you good measure, pressed down, shaken together and running over, and will be poured into your lap. For with the measure you use, it will be measured to you" (Lk.6:38). As you honor this law, you will be favored with the ability to get wealth. As you become successful, you will feel the rich feelings of wealth, smell the fragrant smells, see the picturesque vision, develop a deeper passion for life, and take productive action. You will eventually get the same results that the richest men and women in the Bible received such as Abraham, Isaac, Jacob, David, Solomon, Queen Esther, Ruth, Abigail, and Dorcas.

In my study of psychology, I have learned that there are universal principles and truths that explain much of human success and failure. These principles explain happiness, riches, poverty, health, sickness, and good and bad relationships. These truths explain why some people have wonderful lives and some do not...why some have money and some do not. Secret KEY: As we receive more than enough, we need to give more.

- If you feel that your life is controlled by other people, your job, your boss, your childhood experiences, your bills, your health, or your family...you will be unhappy most of the time. The victim complex is not the answer. No one needs to feel helpless. Antidote: Believe! Believe in yourself...in God...Church...America...your family. Believe with passion and conviction. What you believe, you become. Scripture says, "As a man thinks in his heart, so is he...According to your faith, be it done unto you."

Whatever you say, believe, and expect, you normally receive. Therefore, if your belief system is fogged up or if your thinking is wrong, your decisions to make money will normally be tainted. Fogged up beliefs are restrictive and limiting. If your Belief System is not based on the Word of God, your beliefs will be distorted. Beliefs developed only through life experiences are usually false. Negative beliefs multiply into more negative thinking. This limits your ability to earn a high income and achieve your goals. Your beliefs eventually become your realities. You become what you think. Therefore, think and believe that you can do anything with God's help.

- You get what you expect. If you expect something to happen, this expectation has a powerful effect on your success. The more confident you are of your expectations, the more likely it is that you will achieve it. As you make the statement, "I believe something wonderful is going to happen to me today", it usually will. Expect the best. What do successful people expect out of life? They think about what they want and how to get it. They expect it to happen. On the other hand, unsuccessful people think about what they don't want…and who is to blame for their problems and difficulties. As a result, they get what they expect…more of the same of what they don't want. Happiness and success escapes them.

For the past 150 years, psychologists have tried to understand the functioning of the human mind. Sigmund Freud, Alfred Adler, Karl Jung, Abraham Maslow, William Glasser, Eric Fromm, B. F. Skinner, and others have tried to explain it. Most have concluded that the way our minds are programmed from early childhood plays a very important part in our lives as adults. I believe this is true; however, our thought processes, words, confessions, values, and habits can be completely changed through Christ.

- "I can do all things through Christ Who strengthens me" (Phil.4:13). As our values get in line with Scripture, our achievements and successes increase proportionately. We will begin to see ourselves differently. Our self-image will change dramatically for the best, giving us the opportunity to excel in everything we do, especially in making money and paying our debts. As good stewards of God's resources, our goal should be to earn as much money as possible so that we can give it away to God and others. QUESTION: How can we help others us if we have no money?

- God has already given us the "power" to get wealth. We just need to do it. As Christians, it is our Divine right and privilege to achieve financial independence and get out debt. "Owe no man anything" (Rom.13:8). Is this possible? Yes!

In the year 1900, there were only 5,000 millionaires in America. In 2000,
there were more than five million millionaires and 300 billionaires. Most of these millionaires and billionaires began with nothing. Millionaires come from every conceivable background. Some are well educated…some are not. Some drop out of high school. Some come from families that have lived in America for many generations. Some come to America as immigrants with no friends, contacts, skills, or the ability to speak English. One thing they have in common. They want to make money and be financially independent.

Most people in America do not think in terms of saving and accrual. They think about spending every penny they get their hands on…and whatever else they can borrow from friends or put on credit cards… sometimes not even thinking about paying the money back.

The Bible says, "You lazy fool, look at an ant. Watch it closely; let it teach you a thing or two. Nobody has to tell it what to do. All summer it stores up food; at harvest it stockpiles provisions. So how long are you going to laze around doing nothing? How long before you get out of bed? A nap here, a nap there, a day off here, a day off there, sit back, take it easy…do you know what comes next? Just this: You can look forward to a dirt-poor life and poverty your permanent houseguest" (Pr.6:6-11, The Message).

What is Godly success? What does the Word say about Godly success and money matters? Let us take a look at Psalm 112 at the blessings of the Just (the righteous ones…the Godly).

Psalm 112 says this about YOU and me:

1. YOU shall praise HIM and be blessed.
2. YOU shall fear (respect) God and be blessed. We have the power to get wealth (Deut.8:18).

3. YOU shall delight greatly in His WORD. Observe and obey the WORD, then you will be prosperous. You will have good success (Jos.1:8).

4. Your seed (children) shall be mighty (powerful) champions, STRONG, valiant, full of courage). They shall do exploits (Dan.11:12).

5. WHERE will your children be mighty? ON THE EARTH…

6. Your entire generation shall be blessed.

7. WEALTH and RICHES shall be in your house. Do you have a house yet? Get one and then God will fill it up with riches. Not only will you have wealth and riches in your HOUSE, but your righteousness will be forever.

8. YOU shall walk in light and not darkness.

9. YOU are full of compassion (love and mercy)…having sympathy for others.

10. YOU are righteous (as though you have never sinned having the right standing with God with no feeling of inferiority or condemnation.

11. YOU have a legal right to stand in the Father's presence just as if YOU have NEVER sinned and sin had NEVER been (1 Cor.1:30, 2 Cor.5:21, Rom. 5:1, 8:1).

12. YOU will show favor to others. YOU will lend when necessary (Deut. 28, Prov. 19:17). YOU will guide your affairs with justice and fairness (discretion). YOU will use good judgment.

13. During a recession, YOU SHALL NOT BE MOVED (Ps.30:6, 16:8, 62:6). YOUR faith in God shall not waver.

14. The godly Christian will not be afraid of bad news. He will anticipate GOOD NEWS. He will confess good news. He will not have an evil report (words of doubt). Why? Because his heart is fixed on God. His heart is established. The Christian shall not be afraid while his enemies are being destroyed or paralyzed. "Let God arise, let His enemies be scattered…" (Ps. 68:1).

15. After You accept God's wealth and money for your life, what do YOU do then? Start, by giving it away. "He is no fool to give up that which he cannot keep, to gain that which he cannot lose." Begin to GIVE to:
- Your families
- The House of God (Pr. 3:9, Ex. 23:15, Lk.6:38, Deut. 16:16).
- To the poor.
- To Godly ministries.

Your righteousness shall be forever. Your strength and power will be honored.

Faith is involved in our *Success in Finances*. The Bible says, "For we walk by faith. We regulate our lives and conduct by our conviction…to God…thus we walk not by sight or by appearance" (Amp. 2 Cor. 5:7). In addition, there are times when we are moved by what we see, hear, and feel. God has feelings. Jesus has feelings. We all do. We need our senses or God would never have given them to us! Faith is only part of the equation. GOD has also given us our five senses to assist us in our finances.

YOU WERE BORN TO RULE:
- It is your God given right.
- It is inherent within you.
- YOU were born to govern and control.
- YOU are either ruling or being ruled.
- The enemy (the evil one) has no power over YOU.
- YOU have the power to rule. "Where the WORD of a king is, there is power". YOU have the resources of God. YOU are a SUCCESS in Finances.
- May the LORD BLESS EVERYTHING YOU put your HAND to DO. PROSPERITY is YOURS. God's blessings are yours. ALL THINGS ARE YOURS!

SUCCESS in FINANCES
By Tommy Franks

What is SUCCESS in FINANCES?
Is it having self-pity or dissatisfaction?
Is it feeling sorry for our reaction?
Is it having a LONG face instead of a smile?
Is it crying the blues in disgrace?
NO…NO…NO…NO!
SUCCESS is laughing in the face of desperation.
SUCCESS is having courage in the face of devastation.
SUCCESS is loving even the belligerent dissident.

SUCCESS is loving even the most impenitent.
Even our critics will inquire
And we will be admired.
Some church goers and Christians vacillate.
They seem to find all kinds of ways to procrastinate!
Some have their heads in the clouds
Looking for the "rapture" as their shroud.
But true SUCCESS is appreciating the BEAUTY that is NOW,
The mountains, streams, waterfalls, or even a brown cow!
SUCCESS is edifying others.
SUCCESS is comforting the sick.
SUCCESS is Kingdom Living TODAY…
That will never be far away.
You can Heal the sick, give to the poor, and captives deliver…
Because Jesus is the Healer and Forgiver!
SUCCESS is enthusiasm.
SUCCESS is being in God passionately involved…
And seeing SUCCESS as a problem resolved.
Go, set people free from the bondage of fear.
Go, activate and motivate those that are near.
Go, see them laugh, play, work, and persevere.
True SUCCESS is to die to self and give your self away.
True SUCCESS is having brought someone into the Kingdom to stay.
True SUCCESS is a living CREATION who is no longer a prey.
Because YOU shared…
Because YOU cared…
This is indeed TRUE SUCCESS without despair!

CHAPTER 6
The Power of Agreement in Finances

The power of agreement cannot be over emphasized (Mt.18:19). If you are married, you KNOW that a good marriage is of the utmost importance in FINANCES. The home is where thousands of decisions are made, especially in the area of money. Money talks…and it definitely matters in any marriage.

QUESTION? How can two LIVE together unless they agree on FINANCES? A man that takes a wife should be in the position of providing and caring for her. The Bible says that a man (it does not say man and wife) that will NOT provide for his household is worse than an INFIDEL. How many infidels have you seen lately? In a Christian home, if you have a lot of "money" problems, it doesn't take very long until you find out that you have a "man" problem. Don't shut me down for speaking the truth! Finances begin at home with the HUSBAND…then the wife…and later the children as they grow to maturity. The following Secrets will assist you in having harmony and success in finances:

1. Recognize MARRIAGE as a Holy Institution of God ordained for SUCCESS. God wants you to succeed in your relationships, especially in money matters. God is for you…not against you. He wants you to have more than enough…

2. When YOU can agree on finances in the home, then money will begin to flow in your direction as never before! Recognize that the enemy hates a Christian marriage. He hates a good financial Christian marriage even MORE. A good solid financial Christian HOME is a POWERFUL FORCE against the devil.

3. Protect YOUR home against negative influences. This may include certain friends, TV programs, certain types of music, shady magazines,

negative books, and pornographic videos. Any of these could eventually affect your money making judgment and abilities!

4. Get involved in church. Get to know your priest or pastor! Get to know your fellow brothers and sisters in Christ. Good Christian fellowship is so vital to your maturity and Christian development. Your money making mental ability will become even sharper and keener as you fellowship and associate with God's kids.

5. Value the opinions of your spouse and other family members. Listen to them! YOU need them for growth. LOVE them. CARE for them. Pray with them. Learn from them. LEAN on them. Let them lean on YOU. Communication and interaction will benefit your whole family in financial success.

6. Admire and brag on your mate and children (even when they do not measure up to your standards). TELL them that YOU LOVE them and how IMPORTANT they are to you.

7. When the enemy tries to come in against your finances, LIKE a FLOOD GOD will RAISE up a STANDARD AGAINST him. YOU must take authority over the enemy (Mt.18:18) and REMOVE him from your presence and territory. Tell him that he is trespassing on God's property. Your home is HOLY. Your MARRIAGE is HOLY. Do not let the enemy play with your finances. He is a THIEF.

8. DO NOT rehearse financial failures in your home or anywhere. Use the financial past as a stepping stone. Accentuate your successes. Allow your Chief Financial Advisor (Jesus Christ) to assist you in your ability to make money! Always see the possibilities, not the problems. FOCUS on the solution. NEVER allow your MOUTH to TALK LACK. If you talk LACK (what you do not have), that is exactly what you will have...LACK and plenty of it! NEVER say, "Well, I just can't afford it. I just can't afford that." This statement will KILL you financially. The moment you say that you do not have the money for something or can't afford something, the enemy will come on the scene to carry out your WORDS of DOUBT. It is called self-fulfilling prophecy or more

accurately "...you shall HAVE what you SAY" (Mk.11:23). There are times when we do not need to say anything, especially concerning lack.

9. Keep some information confidential between you and your mate. Sometimes, it is nobody's business how much you paid or did NOT pay for something. Tell them that you would rather NOT divulge that information to them. Try to do it in a tactful way. Neither is it anyone's business how much money you have in your various bank accounts. USE DISCRETION.

10. Make investments in one another in the home. Educate each other. BUY GOOD BOOKS! Give gifts to each other in the HOME! If YOU can give in the home, YOU ARE a GIVER! Charity (love) truly begins in the HOME! Invest time in each other. INVEST time in your children. GO PLACES TOGETHER. Do things TOGETHER! ENJOY each other. SPOIL each other!

11. NEVER QUIT...NEVER GIVE UP...YOU CAN MAKE IT TOGETHER as a happy and prosperous family. Minimize the problems and maximize the opportunities. Never say that you cannot afford something. With God's help, you can afford anything in His Kingdom. You are the APPLE of God's Eye. He wants you to PROSPER in every area of your life, especially in finances. If you can prosper on the home front...you can prosper anywhere and have incredible success in finances.

"My people are (broke, destroyed financially) for lack of knowledge" (Hos.4:6).
    "Give and it shall be given unto you..." (Lk. 6:38).
    "...he that sows bountifully shall reap bountifully" (2 Cor. 9:6).
    "Wealth and riches shall be in YOUR house..." (Ps. 112:3).
    "...whatever you do shall prosper" (Ps.1:3).
    "Be ye doers of the WORD..." (James 1:22).

REMEMBER the following when in agreement for finances:

1. KNOW that God wants YOU to prosper.
2. Desire to prosper.

3. Use God's system of tithing and giving.

4. SEE YOURSELF prospering.

5. Speak God's WORD.

6. It takes a prosperous attitude to reap a financial HARVEST.

7. Jesus became poor so that YOU could be RICH.

8. God wants you to walk in victory in all areas of your life.

9. PRAY your DESIRE, NOT your PROBLEM.

10. Meditate on and speak your desire.

11. Believe God's WORD and verbally speak it.

12. God created man/woman to have dominion (right and power to govern and control) over their finances.

13. We have an everlasting covenant with our FATHER.

14. SEEK the SOURCE, NOT the THINGS.

15. LOVE PEOPLE and USE THINGS.

16. Choose to serve God and make riches serve YOU!

17. Words are seeds in the spirit world. They bring to pass the things spoken.

18. Words are powerful because your tongue governs your heart. To prosper in any area, you must practice tongue control or be hung by the tongue!

19. God's WORD is supernatural ability.

20. God considers any STATEMENT that DISAGREES with HIS WORD to be an EVIL REPORT.

21. IDLE words usually contradict God's WORD.

22. Never speak anything that is not YOUR will.

23. Learn the vocabulary of silence. Practice speaking only what God says and only what YOU desire to come to pass.

25. YOU ARE THE ONE WHO DETERMINES YOUR SUCCESS.

26. Speak abundance before the need arises.

27. Resist lack like YOU would resist the devil. The words YOU speak are powerful.

In 1977, I was living in Huntsville, Alabama. I had $12 to my name! That was it. God spoke to me and said, "Tommy, go out and celebrate tonight. Celebrate the breakthrough of MONEY that I will give to YOU shortly." I went out to one of the best restaurants in town and had a steak with all the trimmings. My stomach was full. My pockets were empty. My heart was full. My bank accounts were depleted. My faith was high. My money was low. But I believed God! Three days later I received a phone call which was an advance notice that "over $4,000 would be sent to me within a few days." And it was so! Within five days, I received $4400. Praise to You, Lord Christ!

CHAPTER 7
The Blessings of Abraham

We have the Blessings of Abraham. As we are obedient in the law of giving as required by God in Malachi 3:8-10, God will rebuke the devourer (satan) for our sake (V.11). When we involve ourselves in the Word of God and become a true giver in accordance with His concepts, we will be blessed immeasurably and God will take care of the devil for us. Our resources will grow and we will continue to give more and more. As we pay our tithes and give our offerings, we will be BLESSED and not CURSED financially because God watches over His Word to protect it and perform it (Jer.1:12). Look at the following concepts:

1. Christ has redeemed US from the curse of the law (Gal.3:13).

2. 2. The sinful curse of poverty was placed upon Jesus just like all of our sins were placed upon Him (2Cor. 8:9, 5:21).

3. 3. Poverty was and is under the curse (Deut. 28:16-68). We have been REDEEMED from POVERTY. Redeemed means: to buy back, ransom, rescue from, to purchase, to pay off a debt, to set free, to deliver from sin and its penalties, to restore to favor.

4. Jesus paid a debt HE did not owe. We owed a debt we could not pay. He made Himself poor so that YOU and I could be RICH. Word of caution: In God's economy of things, if we decide to be selfish with what God has given to us, our greed and avarice will take us further than we want to go...keep us longer than we want to stay...and charge us more than we want to pay!

5.   As we practice the habit of "giving", the devourer becomes more fearful and frustrated because the Believer is getting smart. She is no longer unlearned about money! She is outgrowing "lack" through reading and hearing the WORD. God's people are no longer being destroyed by the lack of knowledge (Hos. 4:6). The Believer wants answers. She is searching the scriptures and becoming experienced in the area of success in finances.

Christians are tired of being sick and tired. They are tired of being broke. They are tired of being sick. They are too smart to go backwards. They are tired of namby-pamby, wishy-washy opinions from negative individuals! They are getting into the Word. They are becoming spiritual Giants. They are developing a Winner's attitude! The true BELIEVER is DANGEROUS to the kingdom of darkness. The enemy fears and trembles when he sees a Believer decked out in her full armor with money in her pockets and bank accounts.

The Believer is starting to BELIEVE. He is now taking Heb. 11:6 and Phil. 4:13 to heart. He is believing the WORD and acting upon it. The Body of Christ is becoming the MOST DYNAMIC FORCE upon the face of the earth. The Church is INDEED DANGEROUS to the ENEMY (devourer).

The Believer knows that walking in obedience brings prosperity. Therefore, he is now in the midst of a great harvest. The Believer is now heir and joint-heir to everything the Father owns. He does not have to wait until he dies to enjoy it. He is learning that he can afford anything that his FATHER has in His Kingdom! Consequently, because the devourer has been totally defeated, YOU are allowing GOD to PROSPER YOU on this earth NOW!

If YOU need FINANCES, confess the following DAILY:

"Blessed be the LORD God forever. I have given and it is given unto me in good measure, pressed down, shaken together, and running over. I have abundance. I DO NOT LACK. My God meets my needs according to His riches in glory by Christ Jesus. The Lord is my Shepherd and I do NOT want. Whatever I do shall prosper. The Lord has restored to me what the devourer has stolen. I shall eat in plenty and be satisfied. And I shall never be put to shame. Whatever my Father has belongs to me because I am His child and whatever belongs to me belongs to HIM because WE are ONE. I am an heir of God and joint-heir with Jesus Christ. I'm a WINNER. I am SUCCESS. I talk SUCCESS. I live SUCCESS. WHY? Because the WORD says that I am. I believe the WORD. The WORD says that whatever I do shall PROSPER. Thank you JESUS. I receive God's blessings NOW...in the Name of Jesus. AMEN."

You are blessed through Abraham (Gal. 3:8). YOU are blessed WITH Abraham (Gal. 3:9). Abraham was rich....in cattle, silver, and gold. He was extremely numerous in goods. He was a millionaire. Abraham's blessings are present tense...ours NOW (Gal. 3:14). The Blessings of Abraham are conditional (Deut.28). What are the conditions? "Obey and be doers of the Word" (Vs. 1-2). These blessings shall overtake you. "Overtake" means: to take hold of, reach, and attain.

The 17 Blessings of Abraham (Deut.28:3-13, Gal. 3:13) are FOR every Christian who truly believes in the Kingdom of God:

1. God has set you on high above all the nations of the earth (V.1).

2. YOU are blessed (an act of adoration, enjoying great happiness, blissful, bringing comfort or joy) in the city (V.3).

3. YOU are blessed in the field (V.3).

4. Your children are blessed (V.4). Your Crops, Cattle, and Flocks... are blessed.

5. Basket and storehouses of bread...are blessed (V.5).

6. You are blessed when YOU go out and when YOU come in (V.6, Ps. 121:8).

7. Your enemy (the devourer) shall flee before you seven ways. He is smitten and defeated (V.7).

8. The Lord Himself shall COMMAND blessings upon your storehouses (barns, bank accounts) (V.8).

9. The Lord shall COMMAND blessings upon ALL that YOU set YOUR Hand to do (V8, Ps. 1:3).

10. You are BLESSED in the Land (V8).

11. God has established YOU as holy unto Himself (V.9).

12. People respect you (V.10; Deut. 11:25).

13. God shall make YOU plenteous in children, goods, cattle, and crops (V. 11).

14. YOU would think that the above would be enough, wouldn't you? But God is extravagant! He is never wasteful, but He is extravagant! He says in V.12 that HE will open unto YOU HIS GOOD TREASURE. Do you know what this treasure is…in the Hebrew? It is a…depository (a place where things are kept for safekeeping, an armory, storehouse for weapons, arsenal, an aggregate of resources, cellar (a room below ground level used for storing provisions, wines, and other items), store (God has a store just for YOU and me. And it is open 24 hours a day. Isn't that great?)

15. He will give YOU rain (V.12).

16. YOU shall lend and not borrow (V.12). YOU are the HEAD and not the tail (V.13).

17. You are above and not beneath (V.13). YOU can't go under for going over. The devourer is destroyed!

God has made us ABLE ministers in finances. He has given us sufficient power, skill, and resources to accomplish our goals. He has marked and provided us with intelligence, knowledge, skill, and competence. We are capable, qualified, worthy, and strong. The LORD has given us freedom to act on His 32,000 promises. We are indeed RICH in and through Him! As we become better versed in SUCCESS and FINANCES, we will know more about our FINANCIAL position in Christ (2 Pet.1:3). We have so many beautiful BLESSINGS in CHRIST:

- God has blessed us with ALL kinds of financial blessings (2 Peter 1:3, 3 Jn.2).
- Our Financial Advisor has chosen us (1:4, Jn.15:16, 1 Pet. 2:5, 9).
- He has predestinated us to be saved, free, whole, and wealthy (Rom. 8:29, 1 Pet.1:2-5).
- God wants ALL men and women everywhere to be saved, healed, and filled with His Spirit and receive His Blessings! He foreordained that all who would come to Him would be saved and blessed. HE is a GOOD GOD!
- We are redeemed from sin and poverty by His Blood (1:7, Mt.26:28, Col. 1:14, Rom.3:24, 2 Cor.8:9).

- The Father has abounded toward us all wisdom and prudence (1:8, 1 Cor. 30). He has lavished upon us every kind of wisdom and understanding. We have the mind of Christ (1 Cor. 2:16).
- He has made known to us His will (3:4-12, Mt. 11:25, 1 Cor. 2:10). This mystery is that the Gentiles should be partakers of Christ through what Jesus did at Calvary. We do not need to observe the Mosaic Law or circumcision. The Christian's circumcision is of the heart.
- God has given us an inheritance (1:11-12, Rom. 8:17, 1 Pet. 1:3-5). We now possess that inheritance by faith in Jesus Christ. We have been sealed by the Holy Spirit (1:13-14, 4:30, Titus 3:5). We are stamped with the seal (approval) of the Holy Spirit. The Spirit is the guarantee of our inheritance, the first fruit, and the down payment on our heritage until the physical kingdom is ushered into complete manifestation upon the return of Jesus.
- The devourer is defeated. We are IN CHRIST (Eph.2:13-22). We are made nigh to GOD by the BLOOD of JESUS. We have PEACE with GOD. We are ONE with God. We are the CHURCH.
- We are reconciled to GOD. We have ACCESS to GOD by the HOLY SPIRIT. We are built upon the TRUE FOUNDATION. We are built as a HABITATION of GOD. The Christian has become the very dwelling place of GOD. We are now joint heirs, companions, and partners with Christians everywhere (Rom. 8:17).
- We now have BOLDNESS and ACCESS to the throne room of God with the full assurance that our prayers are being answered, and FAITH in Christ that He is ever making intercession for us (Heb. 7:25, 12:2, 10:19). We are filled with His Spirit and we walk in the Spirit. We give thanks always to God. We submit ourselves one to another. We have the Blessings of Abraham.

CHAPTER 8
God Wants You to Have Abundance…More Than Enough…

God wants YOU to have money and LOTS of it (Mt.6:32-33, 7:9, 2 Chr. 1:12, Ps. 35:27). HE takes pleasure in your prosperity (3 Jn.2, Deut. 8:18). Wealth is simply having more than enough… Learn how to receive.

Expect to have wealth. Think wealth. Talk wealth. Cut yourself loose from losers. Surround yourself with winners. Winners and people of wealth walk their talk. They expect a return on their giving. They are givers and they KNOW how to receive. The wealthy Christian is HAPPY. She feels good about herself. She does good things and the LORD rewards her (Eph.6:8). She is NOT afraid to ask for advice (Prov. 24:6). She is merciful and forgiving. She spends money wisely, saves wisely, and gives wisely.

Likewise, as a Christian of Godly means, you should expect financial Miracles. Miracles of financial wealth happen to people who need them, want them, and reach out for them. They are all around YOU…yours for the taking. Define the financial miracle you want and then go for it. YOU will receive it if you faint not.

You were born to be wealthy! God made you to have wealth. You were born to taste the honey and drink the refreshing milk that God has already given to you. You were born to love, to live forever, and to be financially wealthy.

Be persistent. Do not let the wealth of God go. Seize it. God will not let you fail. YOU are Heaven's favorite product. You are the apple of God's eye. You are bone of His bone, body of His body, flesh of His flesh, and His Spirit is within you (Eph. 5:30). The money is yours for the taking. YOU can make it, receive it, and spend it. It's YOURS! You are linked up with God. You are God-conscious instead sin-conscious. You are aware of faith-filled words and what they will do for you. Receive what God has to offer.

YOU have become a successful Christian! Circumstances do not dominate you. You love Jesus. You love others. You are obedient to His WORD. You look for wealth. You find it. You encourage yourself and others (1Sam. 30:6).

1. Believe in yourself...Listen...Accept differences in other people.

2. Do not be afraid to stick your neck out. Be BOLD as a lion (Pr.28:1).

3. You have a legal right to use HIS NAME...You are clothed in His righteousness...filled with His love and life.

4. The Greater one lives in YOU. You are free!

5. You have been restored...You prosper in whatever YOU do (Ps.1:3).

God teaches YOU to profit (Isa. 48:17). WHAT YOU MAKE HAPPEN FOR OTHERS, GOD WILL MAKE HAPPEN FOR YOU. YOU were BORN to RULE (dominate circumstances). Let's take a look at Psalm 8:1-6:

- His Name is excellent throughout the whole earth and the heavens. He is the Commander-in-Chief of the universe! He has placed His Word above His Name (Ps. 138:2). God has ordained STRENGTH for us. Wherever we are...GOD IS. He has given us PURPOSE, IDENTITY, SECURITY, ACCEPTANCE, and WISDOM.

- "...but the people that do know their God shall be strong and do exploits (mighty acts or deeds of achievement)" (Dan.11:32).

- What is man? I'll tell YOU who man is. He is the APPLE of God's eye. He is the express image of God...bone of His bone...flesh of His flesh...body of His Body and the blood of Jesus flows within his life. He is a shade lower than God! He is FEARFULLY and WONDERFULLY MADE…a person OF DISTINCTION (Ps. 139:14).

- YOU are the MASTERPIECE and CREATION of GOD ALMIGHTY! You are the best product that Heaven ever produced.
- YOU were created a little "lower than God…" (Jn. 10:34). You are crowned with glory and honor. You are CROWNED with success.
- DOMINION means: to rule, govern, and the right and power to govern and control. You are seated with him (Eph. 2:6). You have dominion over every thing that walks, crawls, creeps, swims, or moves (Gen. 1:26).

God wants you to have abundance. "The blessing of the Lord makes YOU rich, and He adds no sorrow with it" (Pr.10:22). This verse contradicts tradition. Tradition says, "Wealth and riches bring all kinds of problems and adverse conditions." This type of tradition is not true. The Word says riches bring NO SORROW with it. The blessing of God is Divine FAVOR, Divine GIFTS, and Divine BENEFITS. And these benefits make you rich. The lack of money brings sorrow, pain, agony, and hunger.

As a Christian, you must KNOW that it is God's will for you to prosper. You must desire to prosper. You must use God's system, not the world's. The world's system is bankrupt. God's system has hardly even been tapped. As BELIEVERS, we have hardly touched the wealth of God. Learn to speak your financial desire. Visualize your desire, meditate on it, and speak it out of your MOUTH. SERVE God and riches will serve YOU.

To have abundance, YOU must practice tongue control. Words are seeds in the spirit realm. They bring to pass what you speak (lack or plenty). Words are powerful because your tongue governs your heart. Your tongue is the pen of a ready writer (Ps.45:1). To obtain abundance… practice tongue control.

YOU and YOU alone determine the money in your pocket or bank accounts. Speak abundance and it will find its way to your house. Speak abundance and no devil can keep you broke. Wealth and riches will be in your home. Speak abundance and your needs will dissipate. Resist lack. Remember, your words are powerful. They determine your success or failure. Agree with the Word of God. Agree with what God says about YOU. GOD wants YOU to have abundance…more than enough…

Think BIG!

THINK BIG even when certain people try to drive YOU crazy. Pray for them. Wish them well. It takes a BIG man or woman to pray for someone who is trying to slow you down or get in your way! The enemy does not want you to prosper and neither do some people! Normally, the person who says that it cannot be done is the very person standing in the way. The reason that many Christians have a little instead of a lot is "they think too small". Learn to think BIG!

YOU are who YOU think YOU are. If you think you are weak, you are. If you think YOU are strong, you are. If you think you are a winner, you are. If you think you are a loser, you are. If you think you are broke, you are. "As You think in YOUR heart, so are you…(Prov.23:7)."

Think BIG. Look the part. Concentrate on your assets and strong points…not your weaknesses. Be real enough to recognize how good YOU really are. Know that YOU are Blessed by God. Be big enough to realize that quarrels, arguments, feuds, and fusses will not help YOU to arrive at the door of riches, wealth, and abundance.

Do not think defeat. Think BIG. Setbacks are only temporary… never permanent. They are STEPPING STONES.

Be persistent. Be tenacious. HANG TOUGH. A quitter never wins. A winner never quits. YOU can be an incredible SUCCESS in Finances.

- SMILE…Notify your face that you are excited and on your way to heaven.
- YOU are going to bring a lot of heaven down to this earth to enjoy and share with others because it's the Father's good pleasure to give YOU the kingdom.

- You are SOMEBODY. God has never made a "nobody". He loves YOU. YOU are the APPLE of His Eye. His Divine Favor is upon YOU. YOU are a WINNER.
- You can be a success in finances. SAY IT (Mk. 11:23). DO IT (James 1:22).
- RECEIVE IT (Mk. 11:24). TELL IT (Mk. 5:19-20, Rev. 12:11, 1 Sam. 17:32).

The Bible says, "SUBMIT yourself therefore to God. (YOU) RESIST the devil, and he (the loser) will FLEE from YOU" (Ja.4:7). Yield and surrender your total being (will, mind, body, and spirit) to God our Father. Take an active stand against poverty in your life. Defeat lack by thrusting it out of your presence through. Lack and want will then run away from YOU swiftly.

You are a Rich child of a Loving Father. He wants you to prosper. You have the right to have abundance through God's wealth. You can be rich or you can be poor. The choice is yours. I hope you choose to be RICH.

What is abundance? It includes: Peace of mind, harmony, health, and more than enough…God Who gives you the power to get wealth" (Deut.8:18). God is the Source of your supply and prosperity. He provides for your every need.

God's finances and abundance for you are not limited. Christ frees you from any limitation. Poverty is not a Christian virtue. Poverty is a curse.

My prayer for you is as follows:
"By faith, receive what God has for you. May Christ bring people across your pathway who favor you…who want to prosper you. May Christ release you from anything and anyone who is not part of His Divine Plan for you. If anyone has offended you, may you forgive them. May you be free as well as the person who offended you. May the perfect will of God be done in your life. May His rich Divine ideas come to you. May you blessed abundantly in all ways. May you prosper. May you be blessed financially…and have more than enough…In Jesus' Name. Amen!

CHAPTER 9
Spending Money ($$$)

Over one-third of the 35 parables of Christ deal either directly or indirectly with money ($$$) or material possessions. Jesus was not against money. Actually, it was quite the contrary. He Himself even had a full time treasurer to keep track of their money. Money was and always has been a means or medium of exchange. People without money are most miserable. Have you ever seen a person without money or resources…who cannot pay his bills…happy or high on life? I have not! I have seen a lot of them "singing the blues" though! We were created to make money and spend money!

Money is used to buy and sell. Buying and selling has been going on for thousands of years. "And all the countries came…to buy corn; because the famine was so sore in all lands" (Gen.41:57). The Word also says, "Men shall buy fields for MONEY…" (Jer.32:44). Ezra said, "That you may BUY speedily with MONEY…" (Ez.7:17). "…But go rather to them that SELL, and BUY for yourselves" (Mt.25:9). Jesus advocated buying and selling (Lk.22:36, Jn.4:8, Mt.13:44). In order to buy or sell, money ($$$) is needed.

Money is not our problem. The lack of it is. There is NOT one thing wrong with MONEY! Money is neutral! Money does what we tell it to do! Money is NOT the root of all evil! The "love of money" is the root of ALL evil. God has given YOU and me the POWER to get wealth (goods, riches, substance, and resources). Now, once you have received wealth (MONEY), what do you do with it? YOU SPEND IT! Amen! Money is made to spend. It is not made to horde or to hide! Yes, we should all save and invest for our future. That is NOT what I am talking about. We should be responsible and invest a certain portion of our assets for our golden years or for legitimate goals. However, we need not miserly horde away money because we are fearful of the unexpected. We need to use our money wisely and for good.

Then Jesus said, "Beware! Don't be greedy..." (TLB, Lk.12). And Jesus gave an illustration: "A rich man had a fertile farm that produced fine crops. In fact, his barns were full to overflowing. So he said, 'I know! I'll tear down my barns and build bigger ones. Then I'll have room enough to store everything. And I'll sit back and say to myself, My friend, you have enough stored away for years to come. Now take it easy! Eat, drink, and be merry'. "But God said to him, 'You fool! You will die this very night. Then who will get it all?' "Yes, a person is a fool to store up earthly wealth...and not have a rich relationship with God".

Some people will inevitably say, "Well, what about all those people in India, Africa, or Haiti? Should we have money when they have none and are hungry?" Are you a sinner just because the man in jail is a sinner or the drug addict down the street?

No! Are you sick just because someone else is sick? No. Should you go around hungry just because some homeless person is hungry? No. Should you be broke just because others are broke? Will your hunger, sickness, poverty, or sin bring deliverance to anyone or help care for anyone? NO! It takes Jesus and money...and it takes a lot of both...to propagate the Gospel and feed the hungry in a dying world! The Bible says to "guide your affairs with discretion" (Use discretion in giving.)

The world needs JESUS! We need to give the world the Gospel. I thank God that CHRISTIANS everywhere around the globe are becoming TRUE givers to the Church and to missions. A servant of Jesus Christ is a giver. She gives to others. She pays her tithes. She gives in offerings. Thus, she will ALWAYS have. She will ride the high places on this earth. Christians who complain about other Christians having money are often envious and jealous of the person who has money.

Remember: Think BIG. Think about God's provision. You were created and designed to have abundance. You were programmed by God Himself to taste the fruit of your labor. YOU were BORN to have plenty of MONEY in order to assist in fulfilling God's covenant. Without resources, missionaries cannot function. Churches will not be built. The hungry will not be fed. The Gospel will not be printed, preached, or administrated. It takes MONEY...and lots of it.

The abundance of MONEY comes from God. The lack of it comes from the enemy. POVERTY shall not prevail against the CHURCH (Mt.16:18, 18:18-19, Lk.6:38). The Church is now tearing down the strongholds of poverty. Our prayer should be, "Gates of poverty must fall in JESUS' Name. Poverty will not lord it over me anymore! I am whole. I am well financially...in Jesus' Name."

To be a money spender for God, it helps to be extravagant...and EXTREMELY unselfish! God has always been extravagant, but not wasteful. Look at His creativity, resourcefulness, ingenuity, inspiration, vision, and imagination. When considering His most important creation of all...man...He wouldn't even spare His own Son! That is how extravagant God is...You are the "Apple of His Eye". You are anointed to spend money! That's right. God wants you to have money so that you can spend it on Godly things...and on your family...and on things that are important to you. Your caring Father wants you to be happy!

You and I are channels for God's wealth. We are reservoirs and conduits of money. Jesus was a reservoir of His Father's wealth. Paul was a reservoir of God's blessings. Peter was an instrument of the Father's benefits. We need to be channels of God's money and wealth.

You are God's ANOINTED. You are SPECIAL. God is on your side. His money is for YOU...not against you. You are redeemed. He paid the highest price in the universe so that you could enjoy His wealth, blessings, and especially money! Lack has no authority or power over you. YOU are in the family of God. What the Father has is yours! Famine and lack are under YOUR feet. All you have to do is walk in obedience and command the gates of poverty and lack to fall. God owns it all... and He wants to share His wealth with you and me! Our responsibility is to speak and receive abundance and set the poor FREE. This is not asking too much when we already KNOW that wealth and riches are ours through Jesus Christ!

Remember, lack is an enemy to God and His people. Lack and dearth must bow to YOU in that Name...JESUS. You possess the gates of your enemy and that includes lack or want. In brief, you have the legal right to stand in the Father's presence with the same authority as Jesus. Did Jesus have a money problem? Did He destroy the poverty around Him? Absolutely! You have His ability working within you 24 hours a day, even in your sleep. You are rich beyond measure! You are MORE than a conqueror. Is a conqueror poor? Your name is synonymous with Jesus and His abundance! Your name is associated with Jesus. You and Jesus as one.

Does money talk? Absolutely! Does money build structures? YES! Does money buy food for the hungry? Does money pay for Bibles around the world? Does money build churches? Is the Word published? Is the Gospel preached? As you give, you are doing the very works of Jesus. The enemy knows that you will damage his kingdom as you give to God's Kingdom!

My word to you as a Christian is to go forth and spend money on Godly things! The door of poverty will come down. You and your money have been liberated and set FREE. Poverty will NOT prevail against YOU, but YOU will prevail against POVERTY. The devil is a LIAR. He has lied to you about money. Money is not evil. Money is a powerful tool that you can use to bring glory to God! God wants you to have money and plenty of it. God invented money.

You were born to spend money! Who are you? You belong to Christ. You are worth more than the whole world. Think about this...How much money did God pay for you? He paid the ransom that is priceless...His only Son. He was extravagant! You are worth more than the entire world! You are His most expensive gift. NOTHING is too GOOD for YOU... His child.

Making money is one thing...but, oh, the joy of spending it! Spending money is exciting. GIVING money away is exciting! Seek God and He will tell you how to spend it and give it away. I do not know about you, but spending money EXCITES me to no end! God's people should be the wealthiest people on this earth. Praise to You, Lord Christ!

Gates of poverty that did assail…will no longer prevail.
You now reign with Christ. You are His child.
Jesus, the Divine says…"Come and dine!"
Money be…lack flee.
Poverty must fall…because Jesus has called.
In Jesus' Name, you are His acclaimed!

God's Money Is Here
By Tommy Franks

God's money is here
And His mercy is so dear.
We are His children so near,
And His love is simple without fear.
He spoke of money, it is quite clear,
It is His way of giving earthly cheer!

God's money is here
Somewhat like a crystal chandelier.
It brings light that will appear,
Especially on the dark frontier.
God loves money for He is the Great Financier;
He wants you to revere and ENJOY His atmosphere

CHAPTER 10
Winners, Losers, and Leaders

Let's take a look at the marketplace and job related leadership. What has winners and leaders got to do with success in finances? Read on. Success in the workplace and marketplace during this century depends on more than just meeting traditional goals and targets. Success in today's complex environment also demands a new kind of leadership, such as: Creative problem solving, visionary strategies, strategic thinking, encouraging and inspiring others, motivational management by participation (empowerment), creating networks of relationships (within and outside the organization), teamwork, and communicating effectively with a wide variety of people.

One of the greatest skills of a leader is to motivate by empowerment… management by participation. To empower someone is: to give power or authority to, to enable, to authorize by official means. Great leaders have the ability to find untapped potential in people and then empower them to do great things. As a US Government executive for over 37 years, my greatest successes occurred when I empowered people. To be an achiever and leader, one must embrace with passion the empowerment principle. It cost you nothing to try it. The dividends are unlimited and multi-faceted.

Losers will continue the same old "same ole" type of leadership that has been around since the last century. It is non-productive for this century! What is the old style of leadership? Fear tactics, intimidation, domination, manipulation, threats, and Napoleon tyranny. They simply do NOT work anymore! Today, as true leaders, we need to empower people. We need to mentor them to be independent. When we create independent people with harmonious independent ideas, we are creating people that will treat other people with respect and honor. They in turn will imitate us and empower others to do great things.

Losers want to hold others down; however, in today's society, failing to assist someone to reach their next level is inexcusable.

As leaders, we want to be released to do great things that are meant to be. If we hold people back from reaching their full potential in life, most assuredly, they will eventually despise us as leaders. Most people want to succeed in life…just as much as you and I.

As we empower people to succeed, we will create incredible people who will be able to do anything that is thrown at them. As you empower people, you are empowering yourself. If you do not empower others in helping them reach their goals and full potential, you are falling short of maximizing your own potential as a leader. This type of leadership is nothing more than a "loser's" mentality.

During the turmoil in the past weeks and months RE: Current Economic Crisis, one thing has become apparent. Somewhere along the way, some people have lost their way…including their moral fiber. They had the power, but abused it. The CEOs, people on Wall Street, and even some Congressmen seemed to be more worried about their own skin than that of the American people. Where are our leaders?

Effective empowerment leadership is the secret to the success of an organization. Leaders influence and inspire others to reach their full potential. To be effective, one must be able to influence and inspire people to accomplish a goal or an objective. When leaders inspire others, everyone wins.

In 1903, Henry Ford became a revolutionary innovator of the Ford automobile industry. He became a legend in his own time. He believed that each automobile needed to be within reach of the average American. Ford wanted to build a motorcar for the multitudes. He said, "My vehicle will be large enough for the family…small enough for the individual… constructed of the best materials…and built by the best people. The price will be low enough for any man making a good salary to afford and enjoy with his family. "

Ford carried out that vision with the Model T which changed the face of twentieth-century American life. By 1914, Ford was producing nearly 50 percent of all automobiles in the United States. The Ford Motor Company seemed to be an American success story; however…Read on…

Unfortunately, Henry Ford's final story is not about positive achievement. His leadership skills did not embrace the Law of Empowerment. Henry Ford was so in love with his Model T Ford that he never wanted to change or improve it. Neither did he want anyone else to improve it. One day a group of his designers surprised him by presenting him with the prototype of a new improved and more efficient model. When Ford saw it, he ripped the doors off it and proceeded to destroy it with his bare hands. How bizarre!

For almost twenty years, Ford Motor Company offered only one design…the boring Model T. In 1927 he finally agreed to offer a new car to the public…the Model A, but now he was far behind his competitors in technical innovations. Ford Motor Company's market share was sinking like a lead balloon. By 1931, it was down to 28 percent of the market… rather than the previous 50% market.

Henry Ford always seemed to undermine his leaders and look over their shoulders. As time went by, he became more and more eccentric and strange. Ford's most peculiar dealings were with his executives and his son Edsel. As Henry became more eccentric, Edsel worked harder and harder to keep the company going. If it wasn't for Edsel, Ford Motor Company would have gone out of business in the 1930s. Henry eventually gave Edsel the presidency of the company and publicly said that Ford Motor Company's future looked bright with his leadership. Yet at the same time he undermined Edsel and criticized him in front of others. The company kept losing promising executives. The few who stayed did so because of Edsel. They figured that someday old Henry would die, and Edsel would finally take over and set things right. But in 1943, Edsel died at age forty-nine. Can you believe this?

Edsel's oldest son, 26 year old Henry Ford II, quickly left the navy so that he could return to Dearborn, Michigan and take over the company. At first, he faced opposition from his grandfather. However, within two years, he had the support of several key people on the board of directors. His mother controlled 41 percent of Ford Motor Company's stock. Finally, he convinced his grandfather to step down so that he could become president.

Henry II took over a company that had not made a profit in fifteen years. At the time, Ford was losing $1 million a day! Ford began looking for new leaders, but because of his insecurity, he would always find something wrong with them after a short time.

Henry Ford II did not practice the Law of Empowerment. Only secure leaders are able to give power to others. Henry II always felt threatened. Henry began pitting one top executive against another until they were either fired or quit. Henry was crafty and weak. He almost ran Ford Motor Company in the ground.

This brings me to another perspective: A leader must be a visionary. He/she must have a clear sense of purpose. People will only follow a leader if they see where the leader is going. A good leader will always have loyal followers. If a leader does not know what he is doing or where he is going, people will not follow him. Effective leaders are trustworthy. They are winners. They want to empower their subordinates. Good leadership can be measured from the trust and confidence your subordinates have in you. If they trust you, they will go through hell and high water for you. However, trust does not come easy. Trust is built on good relationships, trustworthiness, and moral ethics. This is the foundation for a strong and effective organization.

Communication is very crucial to empowerment and effective leadership. Vision, goals, knowledge, and technical expertise must be clearly communicated and imparted to all the people in organization. Communication is only part of the solution and equation. The other part of this is trust. If the trust level is low, it is very difficult to communicate your vision and messages to the employees.

One of the greatest leaders of this nation was truly gifted at giving his power and authority to others. His name: Abraham Lincoln. Lincoln was truly a leader in the arena of empowerment. He knew who he was. He never doubted who he was or his abilities. His security as a leader can be seen in his selection of his cabinet. Most presidents surround themselves with old cronies…not Lincoln. At a time of turmoil for the country when contrasting voices were many, Lincoln brought together a group of leaders who would unify his party and bring strength through diversity and mutual challenge. He deliberately surrounded himself with disappointed antagonists. It seemed like disaster was imminent. However, Lincoln wanted advice from men stronger than himself. He had no fear of being crushed or overridden by these men. Lincoln lived by the Law of Empowerment. His security enabled him to give his power away. Why was Lincoln able to stand strongly during the Civil War and continue to give power to others? Why?

For one thing, he knew who he was. He knew where he was going. He was a man of vision. He had a clear sense of purpose. He was a winner.

People will only follow a leader if they know where he/she is going. A leader must always have loyal followers. If you have no followers, you are not a leader. If you don't know what you're doing or where you're going, people will not follow you.

Lincoln's ability to empower others played a major role in his relationship with his generals during the Civil War. In the beginning, he had trouble finding worthy recipients of his confidence. When the Southern states seceded, the finest generals in the land went south to serve the Confederacy. But Lincoln never lost hope nor did he neglect to give his leaders power and freedom…even when they failed miserably… and they did often!

For example, in June of 1863, Lincoln put the command of the Army of the Potomac into the hands of General George G. Meade. Lincoln hoped that he would do a better job than the two preceding generals Ambrose E. Burnside and Joseph Hooker. Within hours of Meade's appointment, Lincoln sent a courier to Meade with the following message:

- Considering the circumstances, no one ever received a more important command and I cannot doubt that you will fully justify the confidence which the Government has reposed upon you. You will not be hampered by any minute instructions from these headquarters. Your army is free to act as you may deem proper under the circumstances as they arise…All forces within the sphere of your operations will be held subject to your orders.

As it turned out, Meade's first significant challenge came as he commanded the army at a small Pennsylvania town named Gettysburg. It was a test he passed with authority. In the end, though, Meade was not the general who made full use of the power Lincoln offered him. That belonged to Ulysses S. Grant who turned the war around. But Meade stopped Lee's army when it counted and he prevented the Confederate general from moving on Washington.

Lincoln's use of the Law of Empowerment was as consistent as Henry Ford's habit of breaking it. Even when his generals performed poorly, Lincoln took the blame himself. Throughout the war Lincoln continued to accept public responsibility for battles lost or opportunities missed. Lincoln was able to stand strongly during the war and continually give power to others because of his rock-solid security. In today's society, we need more Lincolns. Most leaders accept no responsibility when things go south. They point fingers and blame others instead of being responsible for bad decisions that they made.

Effective leaders are also intuitive (very perceptive and discerning). They have the knack (flair) for making successful decisions. Some leaders are naturally gifted with this trait, but others learn it and develop it through experiences. One thing is for certain…when it comes to effective leadership…you must have intuition. Intuition aids in successful decision-making.

Being a leader of empowerment is not about you. It is not about what you know. A lot of Harvard graduates are currently unemployed. They are highly knowledgeable…but still without a job. You as a leader…are a reflection of the people who follow you. You are not a one-man show. You are not a self-made hero. Empowerment is about recognizing and taking advantage of the skills and talents of different people in order to form a more cohesive and productive unit.

A leader of empowerment has the innate ability to listen. One of the qualities of a leader who is looking to have success and gain the respect from employees is the ability to listen. Sometimes, this means taking opinions into consideration that may be contrary to yours. Remember: Only Secure Leaders Give Power to Others.

Remember the Fords. They failed to abide by the Law of Empowerment. Rather than finding leaders and building them up, they would undermine them…because of their own insecurity.

Theodore Roosevelt once said, "The best executive is the one who has the sense to pick good men to do what he wants done and the self-restraint to keep from meddling with them while they do it."

Only empowered people can reach their full potential. When a leader will not empower others, he/she creates barriers within the organization that people cannot overcome and this is a no-win situation. If the barriers remain long enough, the people simply give up…or they move to another organization where they can maximize their potential.

The number one enemy of empowerment is the desire for job security. A weak and pathetic leader fears…that if he helps his subordinates, he will become replaceable. Isn't that what empowerment is all about… making ourselves expendable? In other words, if we are able to continually empower others and help them develop so that they become capable of taking over our jobs, we then become incredibly valuable to the organization. We get promoted into higher paying positions. We become essential and indispensable. This is the paradox and paradigm of the Law of Empowerment! Over the past 37 years, I have trained and empowered many of my replacements…and they loved me for it…and so did the organization.

By nature, people normally protest change; however, empowerment constantly brings change because it encourages people to grow and innovate. Change is the price of progress. People gain their personal value and self-esteem from their work or position. Threaten them with change and you threaten their self-worth. On the other hand, change can be a stimulus in a person's life. It can make a difference and influence them to move forward.

Only secure leaders are able to give themselves away. Great things happen when you give yourself away and give others the credit. This is the Law of Empowerment in action. When you lead from your heart in helping others, you will soon do away with the need of your job...But let me tell you...leaders like that are never out of a job...never out of followers. Strange as it sounds, great leaders gain authority by giving it away. Losers can not fathom this type of thinking.

What is the key to empowering others? It is believing in yourself and people. You will truly be blessed and happy in believing in others... empowering them and pushing them up. I have had the privilege of promoting people for 37 years within the US Government. Promoting others has been my greatest joy. Read on...

Scripturally, you and I were BORN to be Winners and a Success! Nowhere in the Bible does it say that God's children are losers. The Word says that we are the APPLE of His eye. GOD has made US to ride upon the HIGH PLACES of the EARTH. GOD is for YOU! HE has GIVEN YOU success and abundant LIFE now. GOD MADE YOU a SOMEBODY (Mt.17, Ps.17, 56, 59, 62, 118, Deut.32, Jn.10, Mk.10).

WINNERS have plans. LOSERS have excuses. WINNERS find the answer. LOSERS seek out the problem. WINNERS are part of the answer. LOSERS are normally the problem. WINNERS say that it is highly possible. LOSERS say that it is definitely impossible.

TWO Christians LOOKED out FROM the Church windows. ONE SAW debt, lack, needs...THE OTHER SAW the super abundance of God's wealth.

In the spring of 1977, I bought my first Mercedes. It was a used Mercedes. When I brought it home for my wife to see, she went bananas on me. She thought I had flipped out! She almost divorced me. She thought I had gone over the edge! She said, "What have you done? What has come over you? Are you nuts? Tommy, that's a lot of money to spend on a used car. What are we going to do with a Mercedes?"

I answered, "Drive it! That's why I bought it. Besides, we will make a lot of money on this car when I do sell it."

Needless to say, we went to bed that evening with tension in the air!

Within just a few short days, I sold the car for a hefty 39% profit. Then, she realized that I was not out of my mind! Since then, I have personally owned over 43 Mercedes'. The Lord is GOOD!

JESUS CAME TO SET YOU and YOUR FAMILY FREE and to MAKE YOU a Success. JESUS has set you free from: FAILURE (Phil.4:13), POVERTY (Phil.4:19), FEAR (2 Tim.1:7), DOUBT (Rom.12:3), WEAKNESS (Ps.27:1, Dan.11:32), DEFEAT (2 Cor.2:14), IGNORANCE (1 Cor.1:30), SIN (1 Jn.1:7), WORRY (1 Pet.5:7), BONDAGE (2 Cor.3:17), and CONDEMNATION (Rom.8:1).

As a Winner in finances, you will have an APPRECIATION for others and a Positive Attitude. You will make COMMITMENTS and have GOOD COMMUNICATION with other Christians. You will have a greater LOVE and SENSITIVITY for others. Your SENSE of HUMOR, PATIENCE, and TOLERANCE for the weakness in fellow Christians will expand.

MONEY will be manifested in your life as you constantly demonstrate the following:
1. LOVE (1 Cor.13).
2. POWER (Lk.10:19).
3. WISDOM (1 Cor.1:30, Pr.4:5-13).
4. MERCY (Pr.28:13, Mt.5:7, Lk.1:50).
5. WEALTH (Deut.8:18, Lk.6:38, Mal.3:10).

6. FORGIVENESS (Mt.6:14, Mk.11:25, Lk.11:4).

7. FAITHFULNESS (Pr.28:20, Mt.24:45-47, Rev.2:10).

As a successful husband in Godly finances, YOU will:

1. Love your wife as your OWN body (Eph.5:28).

2. LOVE your wife WITH AFFECTION (Col.3:19).

3. GIVE honor to your wife so that your prayers are not HINDERED (1 Pet.3:7).

4. Provide for YOUR family (1Tim.5:8).

5. Leave your mother and father and cleave to your wife (Gen.2:24).

6. CHERISH your wife, even as JESUS cherishes the Church (Eph.5:29).

7. Be faithful to your wife and be ready to forgive her when she burns the toast or goes on an all day shopping spree (Mt.5:27-28, Eph.4:32).

As a successful Christian wife in finances, you will: Esteem, admire, and LOVE your husband (1 Pet.3:1-4, Eph.5:33). Did you notice how short your list is?

Regardless of whether you are the husband or the wife, Success will come to you as you FEEL good about YOURSELF. You will have goals. You will study the WORD! YOU will attend Church faithfully. You will spend quality time with quality people. You will INVEST in your mind and spirit by reading GOOD books (such as the one you are NOW reading). And you will listen to GOOD preaching to help you grow and renew your mind. You will use TIME wisely. YOU will be teachable!

YOU were made for Greatness and Success. YOU were made for prominence. You were made to soar like an eagle, not as a chicken in the barnyard eating chicken feed. YOU were made for excellence. YOU were made to:

1. DOMINATE your circumstances.

2. Have dominion (right and power to govern and control).

3. Be the VICTOR...not the victim.

4. Be a GIVER...not a taker.

5. LOVE...and to be loved.

6. Be happy…and filled with JOY.
7. Fellowship with God…and HIS children.

Pray this prayer with me right NOW. "Father, I thank you that I am PRECIOUS in Your Eyes…that You LOVE me…that You CARE about ME. You want me to PROSPER. Thank You, LORD. I know that I am the APPLE of Your Eye…that You will NEVER leave me nor forsake me. I am so SPECIAL to You and Your Kingdom. You have made me a Winner! I am a SUCCESS! I am Your CHILD and part of Your Family FOREVER! Thank You Lord…in Jesus' Name."

SUCCESS in Finances is NOW yours. Doesn't it feel GOOD to take back what the enemy has stolen from you? You will never be the same again! You will become a mighty Christian Soldier in the area of financial success. You will seize and rightfully take the MONEY that belongs to you and your family. "…The violent take it by force" (Mt.11:12).

Joel said to be glad and rejoice in the Lord. He said that our floors (storage areas in our homes and throughout the earth) and vats (containers for liquids) would overflow (Joel 2:24). God also said through Prophet Joel, "I will restore to YOU the years that the locusts have eaten, the cankerworm, and the caterpillar, and the palmerworm…which I sent (allowed) among you" (Joel 2:25). ALL of God's 32,000 promises apply to you and me as children of God. RECEIVE! You can take back what the enemy has stolen. And this is only the beginning! Praise to you Lord Christ.

"And YOU shall eat in PLENTY, and be SATISFIED, and praise the Name of the Lord…" (Joel 2:26). There is no hunger for you because you belong to the family of God. Abundance (more than enough) is YOURS. You will not lack. The Lord is your Shepherd. God has been so GOOD to you. He will never let you down. You will not be put to shame. God loves you so very much!

I am so excited! You and I are incredible Winners! Period! We do not follow the crowd. The crowd follows us. We take an independent stand that does not go along with tradition. Some people say that you cannot live for God and be wealthy, but they do not KNOW our God!

The resources of God belong to you and your family today! We no longer have the "loser syndrome". Poverty has lost his power over us. God's wealth and MONEY are ours!

We command poverty to leave and it leaves. We refuse to be broke ever again! Our bank accounts overflow with money in order that we may GIVE to the Kingdom of God as never before. We refuse to be bound. Religious demons of lack and poverty have tried unsuccessfully to bind us and make us bankrupt like the world's system. We serve a Greater One…Jesus!

Jesus won the war with satan. Jesus won the war on poverty! Jesus won the war on sin. As Winners, when we speak, people listen. We are NOT arrogant, but humble. We know where we have been. We were once in sin, miry clay, and even poverty, but now we are on our way to Planet Heaven. We refuse mediocrity! Our plans are in place. They were initiated 2000 years ago by our Commander-in-Chief, Jesus. He has taught us wisdom about finances.

Our mission (since we have chosen to accept it) is to go in and possess the land, finances, money, territory, community, county, state, nation, and world for Jesus Christ. God has given us the Kingdom. SUCCESS is ours. We are Winners!

We give up NO GROUND! We continue to march. We seize our finances and possess them. This is the Father's will. Why? To establish His Covenant!

We are tearing down the strongholds of the forces of darkness. We walk in and set the captives free! We take back what the devil has stolen from us. As Winners, we are bold and fearless! We are armed with the Word of God and are dangerous to the kingdom of darkness. Why? Because JESUS totally defeated the enemy 2000 years ago. When the enemy attempts to attack us, he will have to flee SEVEN different ways. There is no place for him to hide. He is a doomed and defeated foe!

Even though the war of good and evil has been fought and won by our Lord Jesus Christ, the Church is still in SPIRITUAL COMBAT…

taking territories for the Kingdom of God. The enemy does not stand a chance. WE are the VICTORS! There is no WAY that WE can LOSE. The Bible says that ANYTHING that WE DO will PROSPER! Praise be to Jesus, our Lord and Christ!

You and I are in the same class as God. Please do not misunderstand me. We are NOT God, but we are His kids. The Bible says that we are body of His Body...bone of His bone...flesh of His flesh (Eph.5:30). And we have His Spirit. We were made (created) in His direct image! You and I are members of the highest social class and social order either on this earth or in heaven. We are in the same CLASS as God! Think about it. We are made in His direct image. God will never die and neither will we. We will live forever either in heaven or hell. We are part God. Please do not misquote me, now. I did not say that we are God, but we are part God. We have Divine status. We are bone of His Bone...flesh of His Flesh...body of His Body, and the Blood of Jesus Christ His Son flows through our veins. I'm so excited!

The real YOU lives inside you. When I look at you from the outside, I do not see the real YOU. YOU are on the inside. You are the INNER MAN...the inner person! When God looks at YOU, He looks on the inside, not on the surface. God sees the REAL BEAUTY in YOU! The Bible says that even your feet are beautiful. When God looks at you, He sees a Winner and an incredible Success in Finances! You are a Holy Spirit Success in Finances through Jesus Christ!

Being a Winner is now second nature to you. You are bold! You are successful! The Word says, "...Be strong in the Lord and in the POWER of His might" (Eph.6:10). "For the Kingdom of God is not in word, but in POWER" (1 Cor.4:20). "Behold I give unto YOU POWER..." (Lk.10:19). "God has not given you the spirit of fear; but of POWER, and of LOVE, and of a sound MIND" (2 Tim.1:7).

Finances come to you. Money is attracted to you! YOU and I are anointed and ordained to bring SUCCESS to our churches and communities. That is part of the covenant. The ANOINTING brings prosperity. The anointing DESTROYS the yoke of bondage, disease, sin, oppression, poverty, and the curse (Isa.10:27). The Word says that you are anointed. YOU have the anointing (1 Jn.2:20,27; 1Jn.3:7). God has anointed YOU (2 Cor.1:21) to be free in every area of your life and that includes finances.

David prayed, "Restore unto me the JOY of Thy salvation (protection, healing, prosperity, preservation from afflictions, wholeness, and complete deliverance)" (Ps.51:12). Jesus was indeed a Winner because everywhere He went, He brought revival by destroying poverty, disease, infirmities, pains, sickness, and death. He wanted people to have more than enough…to be wealthy and healthy. Jesus destroyed and demolished disease, poverty, and death. He literally brought heaven to earth.

You asked, "Well, why are people still poor?" Fair enough…now let me ask you a question. Why are people still unsaved?

He told us that we could NOW do anything (Mt.17:20). He told us that we NOW have all power over the enemy and that includes power over our finances. Jesus said that it is the Father's GOOD PLEASURE to give us the kingdom (Lk.12:32). As long as we are obedient, He told us that we could have what we say and desire.

Jesus gave us a positive mental, spiritual, and physical attitude. No longer are we inferior. We are well indeed. The Word says that someday, we will even judge the angels (1 Cor.6:3). That's how important we are to God!

Jesus brought FINANCES and gave us back our dignity, self-esteem, and righteousness (right standing with God). He gave us the Holy Spirit to comfort and assist us at all times. He did it all for us. Oh, the mercy of the Lord is so great and everlasting. He has set us FREE indeed!

Many times the Lord will say, "Tommy, stand still and see the salvation of the Lord. Do NOT fear. I am with you. Be not afraid. The battle is not yours, but Mine. Cast ALL your cares, anxieties, and reservations upon Me. I am God and will smite and destroy the enemy before your face. Be obedient and you shall eat the fat of the land. No good thing will I withhold from you, MY CHILD." This type of thing excites me!

Today, we take Jesus' place on this earth as the Church. We go forth and erase darkness and sin through His blood. We destroy poverty, disease, sickness, and pain throughout the earth. As Jesus RAZED (tore down) hell 2000 years ago, we raze (demolish) hell today through His Name. WE have BECOME Winners in FINANCES! We have success in finances!

CHAPTER 11
Debt Free at Last

What is the secret? You do not have to be in debt. YOU were born from your mother's womb to have wealth! Begin to see yourself out of debt and wealthy. Think BIG. Broaden your horizons. Jesus looks at you as a precious jewel in His treasury. You are priceless to Him. He also sees you filled with His power and your pockets filled money and His resources…HE loves YOU so MUCH. He has commissioned you to go forth and do His will on this earth. Jesus said, "…All power is given unto Me in heaven and in earth. Go therefore and…" (Mt.28:18-19). Get wealth. Receive wealth. Give it away!

Remember, the word "RAZE" means: to tear down completely, demolish, leave destitute, uncover, make naked, erase, and destroy. "For this purpose the Son of God was manifested, that He might destroy the works of the devil (to include poverty and lack)" (1 Jn.3:8).

Jesus came to destroy poverty, sin, sickness, disease, darkness, fear, hate, greed, murder, drug addiction, adultery, death, demon possession, and anything that would hinder us from being totally FREE, wealthy, and whole.

I remember the first bicycle that I ever owned. It was a 24 inch, blue in color, used bicycle. I did not have any money, but my father did; therefore, I talked him into loaning me the green backs ($20) to buy it. As an eight year old boy in 1954, that was a lot of money for me. It took me about six months to repay him. I sold newspapers, watermelons, mowed lawns, and did other menial jobs to earn the money. Finally, when the bike was paid off, I felt so good inside. I actually felt successful…and free…free from that "large debt" that I had owed. Even today, I still feel good when a debt is paid in full.

Jesus wants you financially FREE…today! You can and should pay your debts. A Christian that has bill collectors calling all the time is NOT a good example to the world of a person who bears the name of "Christian". To strive toward paying all of your debts is a good thing… being debt free is even better!

When Jesus was upon this earth in the flesh, He went about doing GOOD which included paying His just debts (Mt.17:27). Jesus was ANOINTED. YOU are ANOINTED. You are equipped to do the same works that Jesus did. You are part of the Body of Jesus Christ and the great Family of God. You are important to God! Whatever Jesus did, you can do it too. Nothing is impossible to YOU. YOU can and will pay your just debts. Success in Finances is yours for the taking!

"Behold, I give unto YOU Power to tread on serpents (devils) and scorpions (demons), and over ALL the power of the enemy (to include poverty): and NOTHING (disease, sickness, infirmities, poverty, oppression, inferiority, spiritual death, sin, mental disorders, and weakness) shall by any means hurt YOU" (Lk.10:19). NOTHING shall HURT YOU!

Paul said that our weapons are "mighty through God to the pulling down of strongholds; casting down imaginations, and everything that exalts itself against the knowledge of God, and bringing into captivity EVERY thought to the OBEDIENCE of Christ" (2 Cor.10:4-5).

Is poverty (lack), sickness or disease a stronghold in your life? Is hunger a stronghold? We have spiritual weapons to combat these diabolical fortresses (Eph.6:13-17) and we have the Power of Attorney of our Lord and Savior Jesus Christ. His Name will bring down poverty in our lives and those around us. Praise to You, Lord Christ!

However, when you begin tearing down poverty, be prepared. You will OFFEND many people by the Word that you teach and implement. "The sower sows the Word…And these are they likewise which are sown on stony ground; who…afterward, when affliction or persecution arises for the Word's sake, immediately they are offended" (Mk.4:14-17).

The ones sown upon STONY GROUND are those who…WHEN they HEAR the WORD, RECEIVE, ACCEPT, and WELCOME it WITH JOY…But they have no REAL ROOT in THEMSELVES, so they endure for a LITTLE WHILE. Then, when TROUBLE or PERSECUTION arises on ACCOUNT of the WORD, they IMMEDIATELY are OFFENDED. They become DISPLEASED, INDIGNANT, RESENTFUL, and STUMBLE and FALL AWAY (Amplified).

People will become offended when prosperity is fervently preached or taught. Please do not be alarmed when this happens. And it will happen! Love them. Pray for them. Be nice to them! Say nice things about them!

JESUS began to TEACH in the SYNAGOGUE on the SABBATH day. "IS not this the CARPENTER, the SON of MARY, the BROTHER of JAMES, and JOSEPH, and of JUDAS, and SIMON? Are not HIS SISTERS here with US? And THEY were offended at HIM" (Mk.6:2-3).

Jesus offended them. Sometimes you will offend individuals by the Word that you teach and live, especially when you start becoming a Success! They will accuse you of all types of things for the Gospel's sake. They will even accuse you of being WEALTHY. Praise God!

In my previous book Sweet Anointing, I said, "The Sweet Anointing gives YOU the God given right to rule, govern, control, defeat the devil, and have dominion over every circumstance of your life…YOU are a soldier in the Lord's Army. The Sweet Anointing gives YOU the right to tear down strongholds, especially poverty."

Therefore, I say, "Go ahead and offend them…by having more than enough. Offend them by being debt free. That's right. Offend them by having abundance…in order to give more to the Church and Kingdom of God. If Jesus were here in Person on this earth physically, He would OFFEND them!" Be firm, but gentle through LOVE!

"HE that eats My flesh, and drinks MY BLOOD, dwells in ME, and I in HIM…I AM the LIVING BREAD which came down from HEAVEN: If any MAN eat of this BREAD, He shall live FOREVER…(JESUS) said unto (HIS DISCIPLES), 'DOES THIS OFFEND YOU?'…FROM that time on, MANY of His DISCIPLES went BACK, and WALKED no MORE with HIM" (Jn.6:56, 51, 61, 66). They were offended.

Many times Jesus offended the people through the Truth (Word of God). So will you…if you teach the truth of the Gospel! Therefore, when persecution comes, do not be alarmed about it. Keep on keeping on for the Kingdom of God. Tommy Franks says OFFEND them! Why? It is better to be offended and go to heaven and NOT be offended and go to Hell!

"(IT IS) not that WHICH goes INTO the MOUTH (that) DEFILES a MAN; but THAT WHICH comes OUT of the MOUTH, this defiles a MAN. Then CAME His DISCIPLES and SAID unto HIM, KNOWEST Thou that the PHARISEES were OFFENDED, AFTER they HEARD this SAYING? But HE answered and said, Let them ALONE (disregard them, ignore them)…" (Mt.15: 11-12, 14).

As a result of the Word that Jesus preached and taught, people were offended. As Christians, if we try to pussyfoot around and please everybody with the message of Jesus Christ, water it down, allow it to be polluted with the world's system, tickle the people's ears with a weak message, and compromise the Word, we will be ineffective as dynamic Winners and Success in Finances.

I had rather see individuals offended now in this world, than to teach and NOT offend them and see them go to a fiery hell. Let us face the truth. The Word offends! Period!

"And BLESSED is he, WHOSOEVER shall NOT be OFFENDED in ME" (Mt.11:6). The man that is not offended in Jesus or His Word is a happy person. He does not stumble around. He studies the Bible and sees the Truth for himself.

Jesus taught as One that had power and authority. He did not teach a namby-pamby Gospel. He was not a secret agent representative of God. He went public with His words and character! He did not believe in "closet" living! He wanted to make some important statements to society. "And they were offended in Him…" (MT.13:57).

Hence, if you really want to be a SUCCESS in FINANCES and be debt free, you must be a public example of Christianity. Closet Christians are constantly having all kinds of problems. Some are sick. Some are oppressed. Some are poverty stricken. And Some of them are even ashamed of the Gospel. Secret agent Christians are missing the mark.

If alcoholics, drug addicts, homosexuals, wife beaters, and child abusers can go public, then I certainly believe that it is high time for all Christians to go public. If this offends you, then talk to Jesus! He was definitely NOT a secret agent of God. For this, they killed Him.

I know that some people get offended by the Word. In my younger years, if a person told me that he was offended because of my teaching on tithing, I would respond…"That makes two of you. The devil is too!" But since those early years, I have attempted to use more diplomacy, finesse, and poise. I do not believe that we should go around deliberately offending people, but the Word of God will offend occasionally by its very nature.

Jesus said one time, "All (of you) shall be OFFENDED because of Me…" (Mt.26:31). People are not offended because of you. They are offended because of Jesus within you. You could not offend a flea within yourself. It takes the Word of God to offend someone! That should make you want to rejoice forever. Read John 16:1.

"GREAT peace have they which Love Thy law (WORD): and NOTHING shall OFFEND them (CAUSE them to STUMBLE or FALL)" (Ps.119:165). If you truly LOVE the Word of God, you will have great peace and you will not be offended to the point of stumbling, falling, and getting all bent out of shape over some issue in the game of life.

Even if you do stumble occasionally, get up, dust yourself off, get forgiveness, and keep right on going. Do NOT even look back. Don't worry. Be happy!

You are now a Winner on the road to being debt free. You are becoming a true SUCCESS in Finances! YOU were born to be successful.

YOU were born for such a time as this. God's Kids are beginning to walk in the realm of wealth. As a dynamic child of God, you are living in your FINEST hour…invading the impossible and doing things that most people only dream about. YOU are destined for GREATNESS. YOU are a WINNER. If God be for YOU, who would come against you? YOU are now in God's class. How SWEET it is!

You have more POWER locked up in you than you will ever need or use. The Greater One lives within. He is all powerful and will put you over. Go forth in courage and be fearless as the Lion you serve. He will never fail you. Think *SUCCESS in FINANCES*! Be a Winner!

True Winners are not those who always struggle to be first, but they are the first to attempt to do their very best when it comes to success! They are the first to see the needs of others, envision a plan to help others…are the first to commit to building funds and helping others…and are the first to motivate others to unleash God's power within them.

Some of YOU reading this book have the gift of finances inside you, but you have never released or unleashed that gift. I say to you right now, let go and let God use you in the area of finances.

You determine your own Success. Man does not. You do! God made you for success, but your destiny is in your own hands. Without God, we cannot. Without us, He will not! He needs us. We need Him! You can choose prosperity or poverty. Some people blame everybody else for their failures and problems. Some blame their parents for their own shortcomings. Some blame their spouses for their shortcomings. Some blame their employer for their shortcomings. Unfortunately, until an individual accepts responsibility for his own life, forward progress in the success arena will cease.

Some will even say, "Well, my business failed…" Let me share something with you, my friend. THERE are no BUSINESS FAILURES… only PEOPLE FAILURES. Businesses do what you tell them to do. If we make bad management decisions, we cannot blame the business or God, only ourselves. Therefore, if you make a bad business decision, get forgiveness and keep on trucking! I have been there. I know.

Wall Street did not fail. The people on Wall Street failed. The banks did not fail. Bank presidents, CEOs, and executives failed. Unfortunately, some of them are still being paid.

Success is indeed yours! Therefore, continue to tear down the devil's territory. Gratification will come, as you level to the ground, such evil as sickness, abortion, poverty, infanticide, euthanasia, and disease. You were born for SUCCESS. Financial Success will come! You will feel much better about yourself and your accomplishments in the Kingdom of God. Wealth will follow you as you obey the Word.

The fresh oil and wine from heaven are being poured out upon you to assist you in making money! The Sweet Anointing is upon your life. Praise Jesus! YOU were indeed BORN to be a *Success in Finances*! DO IT! Now that you have begun to accept your tremendous responsibilities in the Kingdom of God, you KNOW that you are a SUCCESS in Finances. You are on Divine Assignment to be wealthy. You now go forth CHARGED in the POWER and AUTHORITY of God. His ability is yours. Your very words are filled with faith, SUCCESS, love, hope, mercy, compassion, and energy. People now come to you for answers. You speak forth the oracles of God. Miracles and financial wonders happen all around you in the Name of Jesus. Poverty hides from you! It runs from YOU! It fears you!

You give and it is given back to you in abundance. Finances and material blessings are yours because of your obedience in giving. You have given and now the harvest is coming into your bank accounts. Even though you have learned who you are and Who your Father is, you are humble and meek in spirit. YOU will inherit the earth. As a giver, you will never lack. Everything you touch prospers! Being successful has become a lifestyle for YOU. It is not a chore, job, or sacrifice, but a lifestyle.

You NOW speak and people listen. You speak to mountains (diseases, sicknesses, poverty, sin) and they move and melt away. People KNOW that you are special and different. They do not know how to explain it, but they KNOW that there is greatness within you. You are filled with financial success! You are a POWERFUL force in Jesus. You are now a channel of God's blessings to others. You have become a powerful threat to the diabolical enemy. You now walk into the devil's territory and knock down the very gates of lack and set captives FREE. The hungry are fed. Needs are met. Money is given! You are in the powerful Army of God marching across this land lending a helping hand! I thank God for you!

A mighty explosion of *SUCCESS in FINANCES* is currently taking place within the center of God's people everywhere! Since the Church is learning how to tear down strongholds, it is part of the solution and no longer the problem! Respect, once again, is returning to the Church.

Now that you have read this book, you are responsible for its contents. Pass this knowledge on to others. Allow others to see the power of Jesus Christ. Share this wealth with others! Do not be selfish. Give this knowledge to others and you will see them set FREE from poverty. YOU are a Winner and incredible SUCCESS in FINANCES! I love you and appreciate what you are doing in the Kingdom of God. May our Lord Jesus Christ bless you and keep you FOREVER! May His Face always shine upon you! Amen!

LAST WORDS

I truly hope that you have enjoyed reading this book. Always remember that YOU and I were born to WIN. Nowhere in the Bible does it say that God's children are losers. The Word says that we are "The Apple of His Eye". God made us to ride upon the high places of the earth. YOU deserve the very BEST that our Father God has to offer. He wants you to be a "Winner" and to have an abundant life filled with joy! He wants YOU to be happy, healthy, and wise! After all, YOU are the BEST product that the Father has ever produced! You were created in His image and in His class! Winners expect to win and they do.

Galileo said, "You cannot teach a man anything. You can only help him discover it within himself." Inside you is a dynamo of wealth and prosperity!

Each human being is born as a brand new creation…someone who never existed before…with the capacity to win in life…each person having a unique way of seeing, hearing, touching, tasting, thinking, and doing things. Each has his/her own unique potentials, capabilities, and limitations. Each is a significant and creative being…creation of God…a real winner! Most people are NOT 100% winners or 100% losers. We all have "bad hair" days. Look at my hair. I have seen a few bad hair days in times past! However, once a person is on the road to winning, her chances of continuing to win in the game of life are pretty good. Winners have different potentials. Winners do their own thinking! They think for themselves. Winners never play the "helpless" game…the "victim" game…nor do they play the "blame" game. They assume responsibility for their own lives. Winners are able to love and be loved. Winners have a zest for life! They have energy! They have passion for the things in which they believe. Winners care about the world and the environment. They are not isolated from the general concerns of society, but they are concerned and compassionate to improving the quality of life. Winners want to make the world a better place! They enjoy life to its fullest!

Martin Luther King, Jr. once said, "The time is always right to do what is right." As the world is winding down and we are getting ready for the future, we need to think in terms of doing the right thing on a daily basis. And doing what is right requires change. As we grow, we change. Growth requires some risk. Risk requires a venture of faith. Faith requires hope. And hope requires trust and confidence in our Maker. Therefore, the decision is ours! We have a vital choice to make. Either we continue in the same old rut…boring as it may be, or we may opt for change in our lives to facilitate and expedite growth. We need to watch our thoughts because our thoughts become words and our words become actions. Our actions become habits and our habits display our character. Our character becomes our destiny. This is reality!

Hopefully, new paradigms are beginning to germinate within us. What is a paradigm? It's a different way of looking at something, perhaps in the most logical and ideal way for the first time. Sometimes, we look at something the same old way all of our lives and just maybe, we could be mistaken about our conclusion.

Case in point: Some time ago, I was traveling down a short road in Lakeland, Florida. All at once, a little maroon convertible car came around the corner in front of me…swerving and going from side to side…sort of out of control. As the car went by, the driver (a beautiful green eyed blonde) shouted out the window, "Pig."

This made me angry. How dare her call me a pig. She was the one losing control of her vehicle…not me! Therefore, I immediately rolled down my window and shouted back, "You big old cow, you. Get out of my way!"

As I continued driving, I said to myself, "I guess I told her." I accelerated and then, as I rounded the same curve that she had just negotiated, I saw a great big pig in the middle of the road. There was simply no where to go. I avoided hitting the pig; however, I ran off the road and wrecked my beautiful black Mercedes. It was awful…Dirt, rocks, sand, gravel, and grass went everywhere! By now, I felt like a jerk. The lady (Karen) was trying to warn me of the imminent danger of the pig being in the road.

The green eyed blonde (whom I later fell in love with and married) returned to the scene of the accident and gave me first aid until the ambulance arrived. She was so sweet. I just had to get to know more about this angel. I eventually married her in June of 2003.

The Paradigm: I should have looked at the situation much differently. What I thought…was distinctly different from the real facts and true reality! As you perhaps know by now, only a portion of the above story is true, but I got your attention, didn't I? We all need to change and look at things through a different window of our minds occasionally. This will bring about growth!

The following financial affirmations will make a tremendous difference in your life even in a time of recession or famine. Affirm the following by faith and believe:

- Through Christ, I am ALIVE. I am ALERT. I am HEALTHY. I am HAPPY. I FEEL GREAT. I am HEALED…I am WHOLE… I am FREE…I am SUCCESSFUL…I FEEL TERRIFIC. I AM PROSPEROUS…I AM INSPIRED…I AM WEALTHY. THE GREAT "I AM" LIVES WITHIN ME…CHRIST LIVES IN ME…THE HOLY SPIRIT LIVES IN ME.
- I BELIEVE IN WEALTH, INSPIRATION, SUCCESS, and HAPPINESS. I AM WHO GOD SAYS I AM…HIS CHILD. THE LIGHT OF GOD SURROUNDS US…THE LOVE OF GOD ENFOLDS US. The power of God protects us. The presence of God watches over us. Wherever God is…we are!
- GOD the Creator…has made us Free and Whole.
- THE GREAT "I AM" IS JEHOVAH-JIREH…God Who provides for all of my needs.
- JEHOVAH-SHALOM is the God of our Peace.
- JEHOVAH-NISSI is the Lord God our Banner.
- JEHOVAH-RAPHA is the Lord our Healer.
- It is my Divine Destiny to succeed in all areas of my life, especially financially. It is God's business to make it happen. I receive His Divine help now.

ABOUT THE AUTHOR

Dr. Tommy Franks is an established author and inspirational speaker. His previous talk show host experience, motivational seminars, conferences, and workshops have contributed to a lot of his candor and frankness. Dr. Franks believes in sharing his wealth of knowledge with others as he lives each day with passion. He is married to the most beautiful green eyed blonde in America…Karen. They make their home in Florida and have six grown, energetic and healthy children. He believes that you and I were born for such a time as this and that you deserve the very BEST that life has to offer. Tommy says, "After all, you are the BEST product that our loving Father has ever produced. He created YOU for GREATNESS and to have more than enough…"